After-School Clubs

for Kids

After-School Clubs

for Kids

Thematic programming to encourage reading

LISA M. SHAIA

An imprint of the American Library Association

CHICAGO 2014

Lisa M. Shaia is currently the children's librarian at the Oliver Wolcott Library in Litchfield, Connecticut. Previously she worked as a school librarian and as an editorial assistant for Scholastic Publishers. Her experience at Oliver Wolcott ranges widely, from managing the youth programs to grant writing. She also tapes a weekly *Books for Bedtime* television show for the city's local cable network. Writing credentials include articles in *LibrarySparks*, *Collaborative Summer Library Program*, *Children and Libraries*, and *Connecticut Parent Magazine*. Shaia also developed and teaches classes for the Association for Library Service to Children (ALSC), one of which focused on using series books with school-age children. Shaia has a BA in English from Western Connecticut State University and an MLS from Southern Connecticut University. You can follow her blog at thriveafterthree.wordpress.com.

Printed in the United States of America
18 17 16 15 14   5 4 3 2 1

Extensive effort has gone into ensuring the reliability of the information in this book; however, the publisher makes no warranty, express or implied, with respect to the material contained herein.

ISBN: 978-0-8389-1202-7 (paper).

Library of Congress Cataloging-in-Publication Data

Shaia, Lisa M.
   After-School Clubs for Kids: Thematic Programming to Encourage Reading /
Lisa M. Shaia.
      pages   cm
   Includes bibliographical references and index.
   ISBN 978-0-8389-1202-7 (pbk.)
   1. Children's libraries—Activity programs—United States. 2. Children—Books and reading—United States. 3. Book clubs (Discussion groups)—United States. 4. Reading promotion—United States. 5. Children—Societies and clubs. I. Title.
Z718.3.S48 2014   JR
028.5′5—dc23   028.55
                      SHAIA
                                                    2013038854

Book design by Kim Thornton in Charis SIL, Interstate, and ITC American Typewriter.

⊗ This paper meets the requirements of ANSI/NISO Z39.48-1992 (Permanence of Paper).

To the past, present, and future children and teens who touch my life

To Stephanie for seeing my vision and making it come to life

To Don for everything

Contents

Introduction

HEN I FIRST BECAME A CHILDREN'S LIBRARIAN I
planned programs around a single book. I expected a
large group of children to be able to get their hands on
the same book *and* read it in its entirety prior to coming to the program. I quickly learned that getting multiple copies of books (especially hot, new books) and
having children read an extra book in between their
schoolwork and extracurricular activities required a lot of time and effort on
everyone's part.

My idea for after-school clubs came after I threw a one-shot book party. The
children *loved* the program. Not only did they want another, they wanted one
centering on a book from the same series. Given my success, I decided to put
together after-school clubs meeting four consecutive weeks focused on a book
series or theme, with topics changing each month. I found that through using a
variety of activities, crafts, and books during each club, children were able to
expand their reading interests and explore different genres and literary worlds.

This book will make your job a lot easier. By reading picture books and
excerpts from chapter books, you can cut your prep time. You no longer need to
order multiple copies of books or read the book ahead of time and prepare dis-

cussion questions! At the same time, you will be encouraging children's pleasure reading. With children's schedules packed more than ever, offering consistent, high-quality after-school programming will help parents see the library as an essential part of their children's education. Using marketing strategies to tell parents what their children will learn by participating in clubs will help your program compete with music lessons and sports teams.

This book is broken up into short activities to make each club appeal to both genders and to keep children coming back to the library week after week. Breaking up the program with reading aloud, crafts, and musical activities will hold children's attention while allowing them to talk among themselves about the books they've been reading. Studies have shown that children who choose their own books do better in school.[1]

I've integrated a musical component in each weekly program, including the programs for older children. Don't stop using music once kids get into school! Music will capture a child's attention and help you establish a routine. You can use musical activities during the program, play instrumental music as children are working, or create a theme song to begin or end the session. Given cuts in music and art curricula during the school day, incorporating the arts in after-school clubs will help children as well as enrich your library programs.

Clubs are organized around popular themes and series books, and are divided into three grade levels: kindergarten through second grade; third and fourth grade; fifth and sixth grade. Each club has a catchy name. What better way to spread the word than to hear, "I joined the Superhero Club at the library!" Weekly activities can be adapted for either a half hour or forty-five minutes, depending on what works best for you and for the children. If you're running the club after school, one half hour might be enough. If you're running it in the evening or on the weekend, forty-five minutes may work better.

I have based each program to allow for a maximum of thirty children. You need an area large enough to allow each child space to complete the craft or activity. If possible, divide the children into six groups (five children per table). To make the transition from reading to activity easier, set up each activity in advance; you can prep the crafts ahead of time by prestuffing plastic baggies or envelopes, or stacking supplies on paper plates to distribute later. Invite the children to begin each session on the floor while you read aloud. You can use carpet squares or rugs to make the atmosphere cozier. Explain the craft or activity, and then move to sit at the tables (figure 0.1).

If you are running the program at a school after hours, you may need to get permission from parents. Most likely your local school system will have its own permission template, but I have provided one if you're starting from scratch (figure 0.2).

Figure 0.1 Sample room setup

Permission Slip

After School Program: _____

Name of Child: _____

School/Library: _____

Dates of Program: ____ / ____ / ____ - ____ / ____ / ____   _____

Time of program: _____ p.m. - _____ p.m.

Teacher/Librarian: _____

a) I give my permission for my child to participate in this program.

_____   _____
(Signature of Parent/Guardian)   (Date)

b) I have been informed that _____ is participating in this program:
                                      (Child Name)

_____   _____
(Signature of Teacher/Librarian)   (Date)

Figure 0.2 Sample permission slip

If you are in a school, you will also need to comply with its rules. Sometimes students are allowed to participate only if their grades are passing or above. Just be aware of any guidelines your school system may have.

I did my best to include inexpensive craft and activity ideas; many make use of office supplies and materials you already have on hand for story time. Many special materials are available at grocery or crafts stores, and you can substitute with your own creative options as your needs and budgets dictate. If you are beginning your after-school programming from scratch, I suggest you purchase the following:

- thirty scissors
- six packages of colored pencils
- two boxes of one hundred crayons
- six packages of washable markers
- thirty glue sticks or bottles of white glue
- 9-by-12-inch construction paper (a package of five hundred sheets in various colors)

Look to your community for funding. Check with your Friends of the Library group, your local parent-teacher organization, women's clubs, and veterans clubs for help. Even if you have the necessary tools to begin, you can still apply to further fund a particular after-school program, age group, or expansion for summer reading programs.

Get teen or parent volunteers to help you with craft preparation and to help struggling children with their projects. School-age children will already know how to use scissors and glue properly, but it's always good to have volunteers on hand.

In order to make your programs a success, promote them to your community. Include program information on your website, in your newsletter, and on flyers available in the children's room or various areas of the public library. You can also distribute flyers to your local school system or e-mail the superintendent a pdf file to link to on the school's community page. In most cases, a superintendent or principal must review and approve all lines of communication to students.

Another economical way to reach families in your community is through your local media. Writing press releases about each of your programs is one way to secure promotion in the calendar section of a print and online newspaper, or on your local television channel. Make sure these promotional pieces appeal to parents as well as children. Promote the educational value of the program as an incentive. After all, parents hold the ultimate decision whether their children will participate in your program. Submit press releases to sites such as Prlog .org. Prlog.org allows you to schedule your release up to two weeks ahead of time, include images, embed videos, and edit the releases after they go live. The site, which releases information to Google News, also maintains statistics, including what words or phrases brought traffic to search engines and how many clicks you have had.

This new approach to book-based programming will revitalize your children's department. Your library will be the center of your community, filled with families checking out books and attending your programs.

Now you are ready to get started. Enjoy!

NOTE

1. Tara Parker-Pope, "Summer Must-Read for Kids? Any Book," *New York Times*, August 2, 2010, http://well.blogs.nytimes.com/2010/08/02/summer-must -read-for-kids-any-book/.

FURTHER READING

- Brizendine, Louann. *The Female Brain*. Morgan Road Books, 2006.
- ———. *The Male Brain*. Broadway Books, 2010.
- Bronson, Po. *Nurtureshock: New Thinking about Children*. Hachette Book Group, 2009.
- Brown, Amy. "Don't Stop the Music! Creating Tuneful Times at Your Library." *Children and Libraries*, Summer/Fall 2009, 36–41.
- Diamant-Cohen, Betsy, Ellen Riordan, and Regina Wade. "Make Way for Dendrites: How Brain Research Can Impact Children's Programming." *Children and Libraries*, Spring 2004, 12–20.
- Levitin, Daniel J. *This Is Your Brain on Music: How Essential Human Obsession Made Us Who We Are*. Dutton, 2006.
- Medina, John. *Brain Rules for Baby: How to Raise a Smart and Happy Child from Zero to Five*. Pear Press, 2010.
- ———. *Brain Rules: Twelve Principles for Surviving and Thriving at Work, Home, and School*. Pear Press, 2008.
- Pink, Daniel H. *Drive: The Surprising Truth about What Motivates Us*. Riverhead, 2009.
- Wolf, Maryanne. *Proust and the Squid: The Story and Science of the Reading Brain*. HarperCollins, 2007.

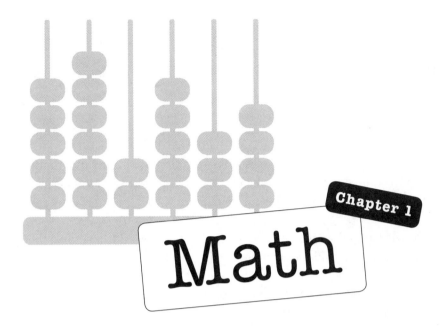

Chapter 1

Math

THERE ARE SO MANY GREAT BOOKS THAT INCORPORATE MATH CONCEPTS. I only wish that some of these books were published when I was growing up—maybe I'd have a better relationship with numbers. The authors of the books used in these programs have done a tremendous job teaching math concepts while entertaining with a story. I love sharing these stories with children and making brains think about patterns and shapes. I hope you will, too.

Numbers Rumba Club (Grades K–2)

Program Publicity

Come to the XYZ Library and do some hands-on math activities. Practice patterning, learn about 2-D and 3-D shapes, and create paper dolls after listening to stories. This library program is a great way to learn how math is mixed into our everyday life. Please call the library or visit the website, www.xyzlibrary .org, for more information.

WEEK ONE

Reading Component (5 minutes)

A-B-A-B-A: A Book of Pattern Play by Brian Cleary (Millbrook Press, 2010)
   – Using simple examples with colors and numbers, Cleary can help teach your children how to recognize patterns and create their own.

Activity: Create Patterns (25 minutes)

Supplies
- colored construction paper
- scissors

Directions

Ahead of time: Cut a variety of shapes (squares, circles, rectangles, triangles, octagons) from colored construction paper. Check with your local school system or state library about using their die-cut machine.

During the program: Allow the children to create patterns with the paper using colors and shapes as a guide. Encourage them to take inspiration from things around them, such as their hair (color, texture such as straight, curly) and their clothes (short sleeve, long sleeve, stripes, a particular color) to create even more patterns. Challenge the kids to create a pattern thirty pieces long or longer. See what they come up with.

Music (5 minutes)

"Everybody Do a Pattern" by Dr. Jean, from *Totally Math* (Melody House, 2009)
- Clap, stomp, and snap different patterns.

WEEK TWO

Reading Component (7 minutes)

Feast for 10 by Cathryn Falwell (Clarion, 1993)
- A family shops for groceries, then cooks a meal to share while counting up and down from one to ten.

Activity: Paper Dolls (25 minutes)

Supplies
- copies of figure 1.1 (Each sheet makes two crafts when you cut on the solid black line; one craft per child.)
  Download full-size pattern from www.alaeditions.org/webextras
- scissors
- crayons, colored pencils, or markers

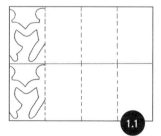

figure 1.2 Paper doll example

Directions
Have the children accordion-fold the pattern on the dotted lines and cut out the pattern of the girl and boy holding hands. When they unfold the dolls, they each will have three complete paper dolls (see figure 1.2).

Music (3 minutes)
"Chant and Write Numbers" by Dr. Jean, from *Totally Math* (Melody House, 2009)
   – Use your finger in the air to write numerals from 0 to 10.

WEEK THREE

Reading Component (5 minutes)
Captain Invincible and the Space Shapes by Stuart J. Murphy (HarperCollins, 2001)
   – A superhero-meets-astronaut adventure in this tale about a boy and his dog, who have to know the difference between two-dimensional and three-dimensional shapes in order to save the day.

Activity: 3-D Shapes (25 minutes)
The following require a lot of precise cutting, so children probably won't be able to finish in one program. This is a perfect program to incorporate the help of volunteers. They can cut shapes ahead of time so each child can have a chance to create a craft. You can always make extra copies for children to finish at home.

Supplies
- copies of figure 1.3 (one sheet has two copies; one per child)
- copies of figure 1.4 (one per child)
- copies of figure 1.5 (one per child)
- copies of figure 1.6 (one sheet makes two crafts; one craft per child)
  Download full size patterns from www.alaeditions.org/webextras
- scissors
- tape

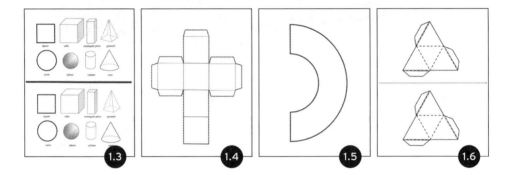

Directions

Ahead of time: Recruit a teen volunteer to cut out copies of figures 1.4, 1.5, and 1.6 before your program.

During the program: Pass out a copy figure 1.3 to each child as they enter the program room. As you read the story ask them to press the correct shape of button throughout the adventure.
- Have the children cut out figure 1.4 around the outside black line. Have them fold each line and create a cube. They can use tape to keep the sides together.
- Have the children cut out figure 1.5 and roll it to create a cone, using tape to hold it together.
- Have the children cut out figure 1.6 and fold each line to create a pyramid, using tape to hold the sides together.
- Talk about the different shapes to help children understand the difference between 2-D and 3-D shapes.

Music (3 minutes)

"I Wish I Were" by Kimbo, from *Laugh 'n Learn Silly Songs* (Kimbo, 2004)
- Pretend to be a cookie crumb, a bar of soap, mud, an orange, and a radio. Have the children shout out the shape of each.

WEEK FOUR

Reading Component (10 minutes)

1 + 1 = 5 and Other Unlikely Additions by David LaRochelle (Sterling, 2010)
  – LaRochelle invents a new math game in this story where 1 + 1 never
    equals 2! Some examples include: 1 goat + 1 unicorn = 3 horns;
    1 ant + 1 spider = 14 legs.

Activity: 1 + 1 = x (20 minutes)

Supplies
  – copies of figure 1.7 (one per child)
    Download full-size pattern from
    www.alaeditions.org/webextras
  – crayons, markers, or colored pencils

Directions
  – Have the children create their own story using the formula $1 + 1 = x$.
    Allow enough time to go around and see what everyone came up with.

Music (3 minutes)

"Techno Count to 100" by Dr. Jean, from *Totally Math* (Melody House, 2009)
  – Dance and count to one hundred.

BOOKS TO DISPLAY

Cleary, Brian. *A-B-A-B-A: A Book of Pattern Play*. Millbrook Press, 2010.

Crews, Donald. *Ten Black Dots*. Greenwillow, 1995.

Falwell, Cathryn. *Feast for 10*. Clarion, 1993.

Franco, Betsy. *Zero Is the Leaves on the Tree*. Tricycle Press, 2009.

Hutchins, Pat. *The Doorbell Rang*. Greenwillow, 1986.

LaRochelle, David. *1 + 1 = 5 and Other Unlikely Additions*. Sterling, 2010.

Murphy, Stuart J. *Beep Beep, Vroom Vroom!* HarperCollins, 2000.

Murphy, Stuart J. *Captain Invincible and the Space Shapes*. HarperCollins, 2001.

Murphy, Stuart J. *Get Up and Go*. Perfection Learning, 1996.

Murphy, Stuart J. *Monster Musical Chairs*. HarperCollins, 2000.

Murphy, Stuart J. *Ready, Set, Hop*. HarperCollins, 1996.

Viorst, Judith. *Alexander, Who Used to Be Rich Last Sunday*. Atheneum, 2009.

Wells, Rosemary. *Bunny Money*. Puffin, 2000.

Calculating Club (Grades 3–4)

Program Publicity

Become a "mathlete" at the XYZ Library. Learn to make seating charts, use tickets at an amusement park, and create animals with tangram shapes. Learn songs to remember math concepts, including "Addition Pokey," "Macarena Math," and "Odd-and-Even-Number Bop." Add your name to the list by calling the library or visiting www.xyzlibrary.org.

WEEK ONE

Reading Component (10 minutes)

Spaghetti and Meatballs for All! by Marilyn Burns (Scholastic, 1997)

– Help Mr. and Mrs. Comfort plan their seating chart to fit all the guests for their family reunion party.

Activity: Seating Chart (30 minutes)

Supplies

– copies of figure 1.8
(one per table)

– copies of figure 1.9
(one per table, plus one
per child to take home)
*Download full-size patterns from
www.alaeditions.org/webextras*

– scissors

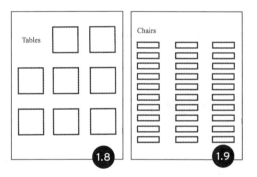

Directions

Read the story to the children, then have them cut out the tables and chairs handouts. Once everything is cut, read the story again while giving the children time to place the chairs around the tables as stated in the story. Provide additional copies for everyone to take home.

Music (2 minutes)

"Addition Pokey" by Dr. Jean, from *Totally Math* (Melody House, 2009)

– Use all your fingers to add numbers to the hokey pokey.

WEEK TWO

Reading Component (15 minutes)
Safari Park by Stuart J. Murphy (HarperCollins, 2002)
- Each child has twenty tickets to spend at the amusement park. Help them use basic algebra to see which rides they can get on.

Activity: Use Your Tickets (20 minutes)
Supplies

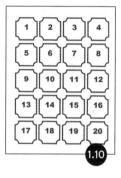

- copies of figure 1.10 on different colored paper (one per child)
  Download full-size pattern from www.alaeditions .org/webextras
- scissors
- pencils
- seventeen cups
- marker

Directions
Ahead of time: Label the seventeen cups with the different games featured in the story. Make sure to write the cost of the tickets on each cup:
- Six tickets each: Terrible Tarantula
- Four tickets each: Wilderness Cars, Treetop Coaster, River Raft, Tiger Wheel
- Two tickets each: Hippo Drome, Elephant Twirl, Bat Tunnel, Rope Swing
- One ticket each: Rock Toss, Giraffe Ball, Snake Charmer, Zebra Run, cotton candy, popcorn, pretzel, soda

During the program: Pass out the ticket sheets to the children after reading the story.
- Instruct them to cut out their tickets.
- Have them use all their tickets and place them in cups to "ride" the rides, or purchase food.
- After everyone uses all their tickets, count each cup to see which ride was most popular and which was least popular.

Music (3 minutes)
"Odd and Even Number Bop" by Dr. Jean, from *Totally Math* (Melody House, 2009)
- Use your body to move to the left when a number is odd and to the right when a number is even.

WEEK THREE

Reading Component (10 minutes)

Two of Everything by Lily Toy Hong (Albert Whitman, 1993)
  – Mr. Haktak finds a pot in which everything doubles.

Activity: Multiplying Pot (20 minutes)

Supplies
  – copies of figure 1.11 (one per child)
    *Download full-size pattern from www.alaeditions
    .org/webextras*
  – scissors
  – crayons, colored pencils, or markers
  – brads (one per child)

Directions
  – Have the children cut out the pot and the circle, then place the circle
    beneath the pot and fasten them together with a brad.
  – Using crayons, colored pencils, or markers, have the children create dif-
    ferent things they would like to multiply if they had the magic.

Music (5 minutes)

"Macarena Math" by Dr. Jean, from *Totally Math* (Melody House, 2009)
  – Count by ones, twos, fives, and tens.

WEEK FOUR

Reading Component (10 minutes)

Grandfather Tang's Story by Ann Tompert (Knopf, 1990)
  – A menagerie of tangram animals appears in this story: fox, rabbit, dog,
    squirrel, hawk, turtle, crocodile, goldfish, goose, lion.

Activity: Tangrams (20 minutes)

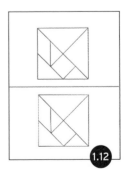

Supplies
  – copies of figure 1.12 (one copy makes two crafts;
    one craft per child)
    *Download full-size pattern from www.alaeditions
    .org/webextras*
  – scissors

Directions
- Have the children cut the tangram into seven pieces.
- Ask them to create animals from the book, or come up with their own. Remind them that they must use all seven pieces.

Music (5 minutes)

"If Animals Could Dance" by the Learning Station, from *La Di Da, La Di Di, Dance with Me* (Hug-A-Chug Records, 2004)
- Pretend to be a dog, a duck, an elephant, a snake, and more in this song.

BOOKS TO DISPLAY

Burns, Marilyn. *Spaghetti and Meatballs for All!* Scholastic, 1997.

Einhorn, Edward. *A Very Improbable Story*. Charlesbridge, 2008.

Hong, Lily Toy. *Two of Everything*. Albert Whitman, 1993.

Leedy, Loreen. *Fraction Action*. Holiday House, 1996.

Murphy, Stuart J. *Give Me Half*. HarperCollins, 1996.

Murphy, Stuart J. *The Penny Pot*. HarperCollins, 1998.

Murphy, Stuart J. *Probably Pistachio*. HarperCollins, 2001.

Murphy, Stuart J. *Safari Park*. HarperCollins, 2002.

Scieszka, Jon. *Math Curse*. Viking, 1995.

Tang, Greg. *Grapes of Math*. Scholastic, 2004.

Tompert, Ann. *Grandfather Tang's Story*. Knopf, 1990.

Tetrahedron Club (Grades 5–6)

Program Publicity

Do you know what a tetrahedron is? Come find out at the XYZ Library. Learn how to build this fascinating type of pyramid. Listen to excerpts from award-winning *All of the Above* by Shelley Pearsall, in which an after-school club tries to create the world's biggest tetrahedron. Who knows, maybe you'll even come close to beating the Guinness World Record! For more information, visit www.xyz library.org.

WEEK ONE

Reading Component (5 minutes)

All of the Above by Shelley Pearsall (Little, Brown, 2008)
  – Read pages 3–4, where Mr. Collins describes what a tetrahedron is.

Activity: Tetrahedron Building (30 minutes)

Supplies
  – copies of figure 1.13
    (one per child)
  – copies of figure 1.6 on various
    colors of paper (ten per child)
    *Download full-size patterns
    from www.alaeditions.org/
    webextras*
  – tape, glue, or hot glue

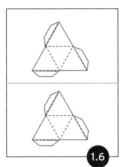

1.6

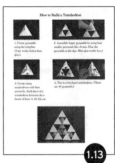

1.13

Directions
  – Review with the children the directions on how to build a tetrahedron.
    Tape works best to hold individual tetrahedrons together. Hot glue works
    best to create larger tetrahedrons; use it only if you are comfortable with it.
  – You can ask the children what they'd like to accomplish in this club.
    Either they can build individual tetrahedrons over the four weeks, or
    they can each create small tetrahedrons and on the last meeting date put
    them together to see how big of a tetrahedron you can collectively create.

Background Music

Do the Math! by Harry Guffee (Pine Mountain Music, 2001)

WEEK TWO

Reading Component (5 minutes)
All of the Above by Shelley Pearsall (Little, Brown, 2008)
- Read pages 5–14, where James Harris III describes a bit of his world and how Mr. Collins and math fit in.

Activity: Tetrahedron Building (30 minutes)
Supplies
- copies of figure 1.13 (one per child)
- copies of figure 1.6 on various colors of paper (ten per child)
- tape, glue, or hot glue

Directions
- Continue building tetrahedrons to get to your goal by the end of the club meetings.

Background Music
Multiplication Rap and Hip-Hop by Twin Sisters Productions (Twin Sisters Productions, 2007)

WEEK THREE

Reading Component (5 minutes)
All of the Above by Shelley Pearsall (Little, Brown, 2008)
- Read pages 15–16 about Rhondell and pages 19–26 about Sharice, where they describe their lives.

Activity: Tetrahedron Building (30 minutes)
Supplies
- copies of figure 1.13 (one per child)
- copies of figure 1.6 on various colors of paper (ten per child)
- tape, glue, or hot glue

Directions
Continue building tetrahedrons to get to your goal by the end of the club meetings.

Background Music

Math Jingles by Mindy Bauer (Mindy Bauer Presents, 2005)

WEEK FOUR

Reading Component (5 minutes)

All of the Above by Shelley Pearsall (Little, Brown, 2008)
   – Read pages 27–29, where Marcel describes his family life.

Activity: Tetrahedron Building (30 minutes)

Supplies
   – copies of figure 1.13 (one per child)
   – copies of figure 1.6 on various colors of paper (ten per child)
   – tape, glue, or hot glue

Directions
   – Have the children finish building the tetrahedron to see how big they can
     create it. Maybe they'll win the next Guinness World Record!

Background Music

Multiplication Mountain by Hap Palmer (Hap-Pal Music, 2009)

BOOKS TO DISPLAY

Ball, Johnny. *Go Figure! A Totally Cool Book about Numbers.* DK, 2005.

Ball, Johnny. *Why Pi?* DK, 2009.

Bolt, Brian. *Mathematical Cavalcade.* Cambridge University Press, 1992.

Lee, Cora. *The Great Number Rumble.* Annick Press, 2007.

Lichtman, Wendy. *Do the Math: Secrets, Lies, and Algebra.* Greenwillow, 2008.

Lichtman, Wendy. *Do the Math: The Writing on the Wall.* Greenwillow, 2008.

Pearsall, Shelley. *All of the Above.* Little Brown, 2008.

Yoder, Eric, and Natalie Yoder. *One Minute Mysteries: 65 Short Mysteries You
   Solve with Math!* Science, Naturally! 2010.

Chapter 2

Fairy Tales

WHO DOESN'T LOVE A GOOD FAIRY TALE? SHARE TALES OF GOOD AND EVIL with the children of your community. They'll want to come back again and again to listen to the once upon a time, the magic number three, and the happily ever after. Learn different ways to incorporate fairy tale characters into library programs to appeal to all ages. Test out readers' theater, crafting, and even singing with these ideas.

Happily Ever After Club (Grades K–2)

Program Publicity
Once upon a time a group of children came together to listen to fairy tales. They met the Big Bad Wolf, the Gingerbread Girl, and the Big Bad Shark. You're invited to join them after school at the XYZ Library. We'll make crafts to take home and hear stories to share with your whole. We'll sing songs and even throw a birthday party for a book character! For more details, visit our website: www.xyzlibrary.org.

WEEK ONE

Reading Component (5 minutes)
Wolf's Coming by Joe Kulka (Carolrhoda Books, 2007)
  – Everybody is in suspense when Wolf comes into the house in this surprise-ending story.

Activity: Wolf's Birthday Party Guessing Game (25 minutes)

Supplies
- small jewelry-size boxes; you can purches boxes from a craft store, use small boxes from book shipments, or create small boxes using cardstock (one per child)
- crayons, colored pencils, or markers
- one set of fairy tale / nursery rhyme cards (figures 2.1, 2.2, and 2.3. *Download full-size patterns at www.alaeditions.org/webextras*

Directions
Ahead of time: Cut out the fairy tale and nursery rhyme cards.

During the program: After reading *Wolf's Coming,* tell the children that you want to throw a birthday party for Wolf. You can use a wolf puppet from your storytime collection for this purpose. Hand each child a different card. Ask him or her to find the child who has another card from the same story. For example, the child with the Goldilocks card will need to find the child with Three Bears card. Once the children pair up, have them color the cards using crayons, colored pencils, or markers.

Each pair of children can decorate one box using crayons, colored pencils, or markers. After the children are finished, ask them to bring it back to circle

Fairy Tale / Nursery Rhyme Card Pairs

1. Red Riding Hood / Wolf Grandma
2. Magic Mirror / Snow White
3. Bridge / Billy Goats Gruff
4. Wall / Humpty Dumpty
5. Big Bad Wolf / Three Little Pigs
6. House / Hansel & Gretel
7. Cinderella / Glass Slipper
8. Beanstalk / Jack
9. Goldilocks / Three Bears
10. Oven / Gingerbread Man
11. Princess / Frog
12. Rapunzel / Tower
13. Itsy Bitsy Spider / Waterspout
14. Sheep / Little Bo Peep
15. Hill / Jack & Jill

time. Have the children place the presents in front of you. Let Wolf "open" them, asking the children to name or guess which fairy tale character gave Wolf the present. For example, if a box has a glass slipper in it, ask the children, "Who gave the glass slipper to Wolf?" (*Cinderella*.)

A birthday party isn't complete without music. You can sing "Happy Birthday" to Wolf before dismissing the children, or incorporate any of the following activity songs.

Music (3-5 minutes each)

"If It's Your Birthday and You Know It" by Music for Little People, from *Birthday Party Singalong* (Music for Little People, 2001)
   – The singer counts back from five and makes up silly actions to match.
"Happy Birthday Letters" by Dr. Jean, from *Totally Reading* (Melody House, 2001)
   – Dr. Jean makes consonant and vowel sounds for each letter of the alphabet.
"Blow the Balloon" by Carole Peterson, from *Baloney* (CD Baby, 2010)
   – "Blow" the balloon to celebrate Wolf's party!
"My Blue Balloon" by Wee Sing, from *Wee Sing and Pretend* (Wee Sing, 2006)
   – Each child can pretend to blow up a blue balloon. If you're feeling really adventurous, you can buy a package of blue balloons to hand out.

WEEK TWO

Reading Component (7 minutes)

Three Little Fish and the Big Bad Shark by Ken Geist (Cartwheel Books, 2007)
   – A modern take on the three little pigs and the big bad wolf.

Activity: Puppets (25 minutes)

Supplies
   – scissors
   – glue
   – crayons, colored pencils, or markers
   – paper lunch bags; consider blue paper bags instead of brown (one per child)
   – copies of figure 2.4 on blue paper (one per child)
   – copies of figure 2.5 on pink, orange, and yellow paper (one per child)
   Download full-size patterns from www.alaeditions.org/webextras

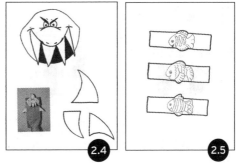

Directions
- Have the children cut out the shark and fish pieces using scissors.
- Have them hold the paper bag upside down so their hand fits in to move the shark's mouth.
- Have the children glue the shark head to the flap of the lunch bag, the smaller fins to the front of the lunch bag, and the shark fin to the back of the lunch bag above the shark's head.
- Have the children tape the fish pieces together to make finger puppets.
- The children can decorate the shark and fish using crayons, colored pencils, or markers.

Music (3 minutes each)

"Oh, When a Shark" by Angela Russ, from *Animal Romp and Stomp for Kids* (Abridge Club, 2002)
- Children can pretend to be a shark, a crab, and an octopus.

Mr. Shark Fingerplay

Five little fishes swimming in the sea

Teasing Mr. Shark, "You can't catch me!"

Along comes Mr. Shark as quiet as can be

And SNAPPED one fish right out of the sea!

Four little fishes . . .

Three little fishes . . .

Two little fishes . . .

One little fish . . . And SNAPPED that fish right out of the sea!

WEEK THREE

Reading Component (5 minutes)

The Strange Case of the Missing Sheep by Mircea Catusanu (Viking, 2009)
- Wolf is herding sheep, but not for the reason you suspect! He's just trying to catch some z's!

Activity: Sheep Mobile (25 minutes)

Supplies
- hangers (one per child)
- cotton pads (five per child)

- string or yarn in varied lengths (five per child)
- googly eyes (ten per child)
- glue
- hole punch

Directions
Ahead of time: Have a volunteer punch holes in the cotton pads near the top edge.

During the program: Instruct the children to glue the googly eyes on the cotton pads to create the sheep.

Have the children tie one end of the string to the sheep and one end to the bottom of the hanger. Now they can count sheep to help them fall asleep!

Music (4 minutes each)
"Pig on Her Head" by Laurie Berkner, from *Buzz Buzz* (Two Tomatoes, 2001)
- Use puppets (pig, cow, alligator, elephant, and skunk) you have from storytime while you read this fun little ditty.

"Baa, Baa, Black Sheep" by Raffi, from *Singable Songs for the Very Young* (Rounder, 1996)
- You can create a "parade" of sheep while singing this classic. Have the children jump each time Raffi says "one."

WEEK FOUR

Reading Component (10 minutes)
The Gingerbread Girl by Lisa Campbell Ernst (Dutton, 2006)
- The Gingerbread Boy's sister is a lot smarter in this tale where she out-smarts the fox.

Activity: Gingerbread Girl (20 minutes)
Supplies
- copies of figure 2.6 (one per child)
  *Download full-size pattern from www.alaeditions
  .org/webextras*
- yarn cut to 4-inch lengths (twelve per child)
- ribbon cut to 2-inch lengths (twelve per child)
- feathers
- pom-poms
- streamers
- glue

2.6

Directions
  – Have the children use craft supplies to decorate a unique gingerbread girl.

Music (4 minutes)

"Gingerbread Man" by Kathy Reid-Naiman, from *Tickles and Tunes* (CDBY, 2007)
  – The story of the Gingerbread Man is sung. (It's the traditional version, where the fox eats him.)

BOOKS TO DISPLAY

Artell, David. *Three Little Cajun Pigs*. Dial, 2006.

Catusanu, Mircea. *The Strange Case of the Missing Sheep*. Viking, 2009.

Ernst, Lisa Campbell. *The Gingerbread Girl*. Dutton, 2006.

Geist, Ken. *Three Little Fish and the Big Bad Shark*. Cartwheel Books, 2007.

Gordon, David. *Hansel and Diesel*. HarperCollins, 2006.

Gordon, David. *Three Little Rigs*. HarperCollins, 2005.

Ketteman, Helen. *Three Little Gators*. Albert Whitman and Company, 2009.

Kulka, Joe. *Wolf's Coming*. Carolrhoda Books, 2007.

Squires, Janet. *The Gingerbread Cowboy*. HarperCollins, 2006.

Trivizas, Eugene. *The Three Little Wolves and the Big Bad Pig*. McElderry, 1997.

Wiesner, David. *Three Little Pigs*. Clarion Books, 2001.

Fractured Fairy Tale Club (Grades 3–4)

Program Publicity

In the land of (your city or town), a group of children listens to fairy tales. They perform their own stories, compete for the funniest fill-in-the-blank story, and predict what happens after "they all lived happily ever after." Join them after school (dates, times).

WEEK ONE

Reading Component (10 minutes)

Once Upon a Cool Motorcycle Dude by Kevin O'Malley (Walker, 2005)
   – A boy and a girl have to tell a fairy tale story together for a school assignment. Everyone will be in stitches when you read each narrator's story aloud!

Activity: Readers' Theater (30 minutes)

Supplies
   – one set of fairy tale/nursery rhyme cards (figures 2.1, 2.2, and 2.3.
      Download full-size patterns at www.alaeditions.org/webextras
   – clock or stopwatch

Directions
Pass out one card to each child as he or she enters the program space. Tell the children to find their partner. For example, the child with the Jack card will look for the child with the Beanstalk card.

   Once pairs have been made, have each pair stand side by side in a line. Assign one child from each pair to act as the princess-loving girl featured in *Once Upon a Motorcycle Dude*. The other child takes on the role of the motorcycle-loving

Fairy Tale / Nursery Rhyme Card Pairs

1. Red Riding Hood /
   Wolf Grandma
2. Magic Mirror / Snow White
3. Bridge / Billy Goats Gruff
4. Wall / Humpty Dumpty
5. Big Bad Wolf / Three Little Pigs
6. House / Hansel & Gretel
7. Cinderella / Glass Slipper
8. Beanstalk / Jack
9. Goldilocks / Three Bears
10. Oven / Gingerbread Man
11. Princess / Frog
12. Rapunzel / Tower
13. Itsy Bitsy Spider / Waterspout
14. Sheep / Little Bo Peep
15. Hill / Jack & Jill

boy. Then ask each pair to make up a story featuring the characters on their cards, giving the partners time to talk about their stories aloud and add whatever complications they like. Allow ten minutes to practice. Then set a timer or clock and give each pair one minute to tell its story to the whole group.

Music (2 minutes)

"Motorcycle" by Wee Sing, from *Wee Sing and Pretend* (Wee Sing, 2006)

WEEK TWO

Reading Component (15 minutes)

What Really Happened to Humpty? From the Files of a Hard-Boiled Detective by
   Jeanie Franz Ransom (Charlesbridge, 2010)
   – There's a mystery to solve in Mother Gooseland, and the detective thinks
     Humpty was pushed. Help him figure out "whodunit."

Activity: Mother Goose Land Who Dunnit? Board Game (25 minutes)

Supplies
   – dice (one per table)
   – thirty pom-poms to use as pawns to play the game (six different colors
     for each table) or thirty coins for each table, used as follows: a penny on
     heads, a penny on tails, a nickel on heads, a nickel on tails, a dime on
     heads, a dime on tails
   – copies of figure 2.7 enlarged on legal-size paper (one per child)
   – copies of figure 2.8 (one per child)

- copies of figure 2.9 (one per child)
- copies of the Settings cards (figure 2.10) on blue paper (one per child)
- copies of the Suspects cards (figure 2.11) on pink paper (one per child)
- copies of the Weapons cards (figure 2.12) on yellow paper (one per child)
  Download full-size patterns from www.alaeditions.org/webextras
- envelopes to put the solution cards in (one per table)

Directions
Review the rules of the game with everyone and let them play a game with their tablemates. Let each child take home a copy of the game.

Music (5 minutes each)
"Humpty Dumpty" by Georgiana Stewart, from *Nursery Rhyme Time* (Kimbo, 2000)
"Humpty Dumpty" by Hap Palmer, from *Classic Nursery Rhymes* (Educational Activities, 1991)

WEEK THREE

Reading Component (10 minutes)
The True Story of the Three Little Pigs by Jon Scieszka (Puffin, 1996)
   – Big Bad Wolf tells his side of the famous story: he had a cold and was
     only trying to borrow a cup of sugar from the piggies.

Activity: Three Little _____ (20 minutes)

Supplies
   – copies of figure 2.13 (one per child)
     Download full-size pattern from www.alaeditions
     .org/webextras
   – pencils

Directions
   – Pass out the Three Little ___ story sheets and have
     children write nouns, verbs, and adjectives in the
     blanks. Have each child read resulting story aloud. Vote as a group for
     the funniest. Have the winner lead everyone in a performance of The
     Three Little Pigs using one of the songs below to conclude the program.

Music (5 minutes each)
"Three Little Pigs Blues" by Greg and Steve, from *Playin' Favorites* (Young
   Heart Music, 2000)
"Three Little Pigs" by Laurie Berkner, from *Buzz Buzz* (Two Tomatoes, 2001)
"Three Pigs and a Wolf" by Debbie and Friends, from *Story Songs and Sing
   Alongs* (Debbie Cavalier Music, 2007)

WEEK FOUR

Reading Component (10 minutes)
The Frog Prince Continued by Jon Scieszka (Puffin, 1994)
   – This story is about what happens to Frog Prince after the "happily ever
     after."

Activity: After Happily Ever After (20 minutes)
Supplies
   – one set of fairy tale/nursery rhyme cards (figures 2.1, 2.2, and 2.3)
   – paper
   – pencils

Directions
- As the children come into the program space, hand them each one card.
- Have them write a story in which their characters live beyond the happily ever after just like the Frog Prince.
- Allow time for the children to share their stories aloud.

Music (5 minutes each)

"Froggie Went A-Courtin'" by Laurie Berkner, from *Victor Vito* (Two Tomatoes, 2001)

"Princess and the Froggy" by Kimmy Schwimmy, from *Kimmy Schwimmy Volume 3* (CD Baby, 2010)

BOOKS TO DISPLAY

Ahlberg, Allan. *Previously*. Walker, 2008.

Kimmel, Eric A. *Three Little Tamales*. Marshall Cavendish, 2009.

LaRochelle, David. *The End*. Arthur A. Levine Books, 2007.

Lendler, Ian. *An Undone Fairy Tale*. Simon and Schuster, 2005.

Lowell, Susan. *Three Little Javelinas*. Luna Rising, 2009.

O'Malley, Kevin. *Once Upon a Cool Motorcycle Dude*. Walker, 2005.

O'Malley, Kevin. *Once Upon a Royal Superbaby*. Walker, 2010.

Pichon, Liz. *Three Horrid Little Pigs*. Tiger Tales, 2010.

Ransom, Jeanie Franz. *What Really Happened to Humpty? From the Files on a Hard-Boiled Detective*. Charlesbridge, 2010.

Rubin, Vicky. *Three Swinging Pigs*. Henry Holt, 2007.

Scieszka, Jon. *The Frog Prince Continued*. Puffin, 1994.

Scieszka, Jon. *Knucklehead: Tall Tales and Almost True Stories of Growing Up Scieszka*. Viking, 2008.

Scieszka, Jon. *The Stinky Cheese Man and Other Fairly Stupid Tales*. Viking, 1992.

Scieszka, Jon. *The True Story of the Three Little Pigs*. Puffin, 1996.

Grimm Club (Grades 5–6)

Program Publicity

Practice the art of storytelling at the XYZ Library. Meet after school to create your own board game, write your own story, and compose an original song. You'll be introduced to characters such as Peter Pan and the Sisters Grimm. Meetings begin on (date, time).

WEEK ONE

Reading Component (5 minutes)

Peter and the Starcatchers series by Dave Barry and Ridley Pearson (Disney-Hyperion)
- Booktalk the Peter and the Starcatchers series by Dave Barry and Ridley Pearson. Peter Pan and the Lost Boys can never grow old. They have adventures in faraway lands and battle evil villains. You'll get to meet Wendy's mom as a child, and learn how Peter Pan and Captain Hook first met throughout the series.

Activity: Autobiography of a . . . (30 minutes)

Supplies
- copies of figure 2.14 (one per child)
- one copy of figure 2.15 *Download full-size patterns from www.alaeditions.org/ webextras*
- pencils

Directions

Ahead of time: Cut figure 2.15 into squares.

During the program: Place the biography squares from figure 2.15 in a cup or hat.
- As the children come into the program room, ask them to choose one square.
- Give them ideas and criteria for the biography.
- Let them work on it for ten minutes, then go around and let everyone have thirty seconds to tell their story. If the kids get stumped, offer a brainstorming session where everyone contributes.

Autobiography Cues

1. bracelet	11. shoe	21. sock
2. stuffed animal	12. table	22. watch
3. sneaker	13. phone	23. magazine
4. necklace	14. chair	24. computer game
5. a piece of paper	15. cup	25. toy
6. rubber band	16. pencil	26. stamp
7. pin	17. rock	27. shirt
8. paper clip	18. stapler	28. sweater
9. pen	19. DVD	29. MP3 player
10. book	20. ring	30. coin

WEEK TWO

Reading Component (5 minutes)

Sisters Grimm series by Michael Buckley (Amulet Books)

- Booktalk the Sisters Grimm series by Michael Buckley. Sabrina and Daphne Grimm are taken into foster care after their parents disappear. They are finally placed with their grandmother and move to a town of Everafters, where fairy tale characters *really* exist.

Activity: Tell Me a Story (40 minutes)

Supplies

- a variety of wordless books, such as
  - books by Anno
  - books by David Weisner
  - books by Chris Van Allsburg
  - Cooper, Elisha. *Beaver Is Lost.* Schwartz and Wade, 2010.
  - Lehman, Barbara. *The Red Book.* Houghton Mifflin, 2004.
  - Rodriguez, Beatrice. *The Chicken Thief.* Enchanted Lion, 2010.
  - Thomson, Bill. *Chalk.* Marshall Cavendish, 2010.

Directions

Pass out wordless books and have the children use them as a springboard to telling their own stories. If you can schedule a real story time with preschool or early elementary school students, you can have the older children tell stories to practice.

WEEK THREE

Reading Component (5 minutes)

Emily Windsnap series by Liz Kessler (Candlewick)

- – Booktalk the Emily Windsnap series by Liz Kessler. Emily is a normal twelve-year-old girl . . . until she begins taking swimming lessons and learns she has a mermaid tail!

Activity: Creating a Flannelboard Story (40 minutes)

Supplies

- – felt in a variety of colors and textures
- – fabric paint in a variety of colors
- – scissors
- – pens or markers

If these supplies are out of your budget, you can use paper. You can laminate the finished pieces and glue small pieces of felt to the backs to stick to the flannel-board. Allow the pieces to dry overnight. The children can pick up their pieces the following week.

Directions

Let the children at each table choose a different fairy tale to tell as flannel-board story. They can use pens or markers to outline shapes on felt and fabric paint to add details.

WEEK FOUR

Reading Component (5 minutes)

Fairy Haven series by Gail Carson Levine (Disney)

- – Booktalk the Fairy Haven series by Gail Carson Levine. Imagine being born from a baby's laugh. That's how fairies are born into Pixie Hollow. Prilla, a new fairy, does not seem to have any fairy abilities. Tinker Bell helps Prilla, and adventures follow.

Activity: Song Writing (40 minutes)

Supplies

- – fairy tale music (see Music, below)
- – pencils
- – paper

Directions
- Play a few song samples from the suggestions below. Assign each table of participants a fairy tale ("The Three Little Pigs," "Jack and the Beanstalk," "Little Red Riding Hood," "Goldilocks and the Three Bears," "Three Billy Goats Gruff"), and ask the children to write their own song about the story. Use instrumental music suggested below as background for singing the words aloud. You can put out your story-time musical instruments for added wow factor.

Music (5 minutes each)
Three Little Pigs
"Three Little Pigs Blues" by Greg and Steve, from *Playin' Favorites* (Young Heart Music, 2000)

"Three Little Pigs" by Laurie Berkner, from *Buzz Buzz* (Two Tomatoes, 2001)

"Three Pigs and a Wolf" by Debbie and Friends, from *Story Songs and Sing Alongs* (Debbie Cavalier Music, 2007)

PigMania: A Hilarious New Spin on the Three Little Pigs by Judy and David (Children's Group, 2000). Any selection.

Jack and the Beanstalk
"Jack and the Beanstalk" by Debbie and Friends, from *Story Songs and Sing Alongs* (Debbie Cavalier Music, 2007)

Little Red Riding Hood
"Little Red Riding Hood" by Debbie and Friends, from *Story Songs and Sing Alongs* (Debbie Cavalier Music, 2007)

"Little Red Remix" by Debbie and Friends, from *More Story Songs and Sing Alongs* (Debbie Cavalier Music, 2010)

Red's in the Hood by Judy and David (Children's Group, 2001). Any selection.

Goldilocks and the Three Bears
"Goldilocks" by Debbie and Friends, from *Story Songs and Sing Alongs* (Debbie Cavalier Music, 2007)

"Goldilocks and the Three Bears" by the Learning Station, from *Literacy in Motion* (Hug-a-Chug Records, 2005)

"Goldilocks Rap" by Rosenshontz, from *Teddy Bear's Greatest Hits* (Lightyear, 1998)

"The Three Boppin' Bears Rap" by Dr. Jean, from *Dr. Jean Sings Silly Songs* (Melody House, 2007)

GoldiRocks: A New Spin on Goldilocks and the Three Bears by Judy and David (Children's Group, 2005). Any selection.

Three Billy Goats Gruff
"Three Billy Goats Gruff" by Greg and Steve, from *Rockin' Down the Road*
   (Young Heart Music, 2000)

Instrumental Music
Rockabye Baby!
   – The CDs and MP3 downloads in this series from Rockabye Baby Music
     include selections from the Beatles, the Rolling Stones, Metallica, Bob
     Marley, U2, Journey, Led Zeppelin, Pink Floyd, Guns N' Roses, Queen,
     the Cure, Radiohead, Aerosmith, Tool, AC/DC, Kanye West, Nirvana, No
     Doubt, Elvis Presley, Green Day, the Pixies, Nine Inch Nails, Black Sab-
     bath, the Beach Boys, Pearl Jam, the Eagles, Bjork, the Ramones, Dave
     Matthews, and Queens of the Stone Age.
Hushabye Baby!
   – CDs and MP3 downloads on the Hushabye Baby label feature the songs of
     country music artists including Johnny Cash, Rascal Flatts, George Strait,
     Taylor Swift, Garth Brooks, Willie Nelson, Carrie Underwood, Patsy
     Kline, Dolly Parton, and Vince Gill.
Mother Goose Rocks!
   – From Lightyear, CDs in the Mother Goose Rocks! roundup comprise
     classic nursery rhymes set to popular songs. "Row Your Boat" is set to a
     Sheryl Crow song, and "Five Little Monkeys" is sung to an Eminem tune.

BOOKS TO DISPLAY

Barry, Dave, and Ridley Pearson. *Peter and the Starcatchers*. Hyperion, 2004.
   (This is one of many in the Peter Pan series.)

Buckley, Michael. *The Fairy-Tale Detectives*. Harry N. Abrams, 2007. (This is
   one of many in the Sisters Grimm series.)

Gidwitz, Adam. *A Tale Dark and Grimm*. Puffin, 2011.

Kessler, Liz. *The Tail of Emily Windsnap*. Candlewick Press, 2006. (This is one
   of many in the Emily Windsnap series.)

Law, Ingrid. *Savvy*. Puffin, 2010.

Levine, Gail Carson. *Fairy Dust and the Quest for the Egg*. Disney Press, 2008.
   (This is one of many in the Fairy Haven series.)

Lupica, Mike. *Hero*. Puffin, 2011.

McMann, Lisa. *The Unwanteds*. Aladdin, 2012.

Shulman, Polly. *The Grimm Legacy*. Puffin, 2011.

Science

TODAY'S ELEMENTARY SCHOOL CHILDREN HAVE MANY MORE OPPORTUNITIES to experiment with science than I did as a child. I would have loved working with homemade playdough and playing in sand and water stations, as many children do now. Being part of a team conducting an experiment without knowing the outcome was always exciting for me. Bring this level of excitement and wonder to kids at your library. You will need a few out-of-the-ordinary materials, but the experiments are simple and involve only a little prep work. The effort is well worth it.

Curious Kids Club (Grades K–2)

Program Publicity
Let your kids satisfy their curiosity about science at the XYZ Library. We'll conduct simple experiments that help them investigate the world around them. They'll listen to stories about astronauts and comets, and then test their knowledge in simple experiments that make use of easy-to-find materials—like spaghetti. Sign up before the deadline on (date) at the children's desk or online at www.xyzlibrary.org.

WEEK ONE

Reading Component (15 minutes)
Strega Nona by Tomie dePaola (Simon and Schuster, 1975)

Activity: Too Much Spaghetti (15 minutes)

Watch the strands of spaghetti "dance" in this experiment. Doesn't it remind you of Anthony's mess in *Strega Nona*? You can recruit parents or teen volunteers to help at each table, pouring in the ingredients.

Supplies
- uncooked spaghetti or angel hair pasta
- tall glass or jar to be filled three-quarters full with water (one per table)
- water
- baking soda (1 tablespoon per table)
- vinegar (2 tablespoons per table)
- spoon (one per table)

Directions
- Have children at the table fill up the tall glass three-quarters with water.
- Have them add 1 tablespoon of baking soda and stir.
- Have them put a couple of pieces of spaghetti in the jar.
- Have them add 2 tablespoons of vinegar to the jar, then watch the spaghetti move on its own.

Background Music

Here Comes Science by They Might Be Giants (Disney Sound, 2009)

WEEK TWO

Reading Component (5 minutes)

Space Explorers by Eva Moore (Scholastic, 2000)
- Read "Ms. Frizzle's Guide to Gravity" on page 17.

Activity: An Astronaut's Parachute (25 minutes)

Supplies
- string cut to 12-inch lengths (four per child)
- paper towels (one per child)
- markers
- hole punch
- erasers (one per child)
- tape

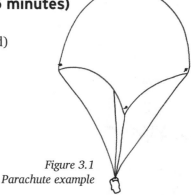

Figure 3.1
Parachute example

Directions

Ahead of time: Ask a volunteer to punch four holes in each paper towel: one on each corner.

During the program: Have the children decorate the paper towel with markers.
- Have them tie one string to each corner of the paper towel.
- Have them bring all four strings together and tape the strings to an eraser (the eraser will be the astronaut).
- If you wish, you can make an X on the floor with tape or chalk and see which child can fly his or her astronaut the closest to the X.

Background Music
Sid the Science Kid (Jim Henson Company, 2009)

WEEK THREE

Reading Component (5 minutes)
Space Explorers by Eva Moore (Scholastic, 2000)
- Read chapter 5, where Ms. Frizzle's class discusses comets, asteroids, and meteors.

Activity: Comet Experiment (25 minutes)
The higher the altitude, the bigger the crater will be.

Supplies

    large trays (one per table)
- marbles or bouncy balls (one per table)
- flour (enough to fill each tray)
- ruler with inches and centimeters (one per table)
- copies of figure 3.2 (one per table)
  Download full-size pattern from www.alaeditions.org/ webextras
- pencils

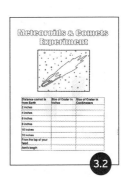

Directions
- Have the children fill the trays with flour.
- Have them place the ruler in the tray with the 0-inch end down.
- Have them hold the marble or bouncy ball on the 2-inch mark.
- Have them drop the marble or bouncy ball into the flour.
- Have them measure the size of the crater left behind in both inches and centimeters for practice.

- Repeat these steps, measuring at 4-inch, 6-inch, 8-inch, 10-inch, 12-inch increments. For added fun, have the children measure from the top of their heads and at arm's length.
- Allow enough time for each table to share their data and talk about the results.

Background Music

Science by Teacher and the Rockbots (Power Arts Company, 2005)

WEEK FOUR

Reading Component (5 minutes)

Space Explorers by Eva Moore (Scholastic, 2000)

- Read chapter 4, where Ms. Frizzle's class learns about the power of the sun.

Activity: Solar Energy Experiment (25 minutes)

Supplies

- colored ice cubes
- copies of figure 3.3 (one per table or team)
  Download full-size pattern from www.alaeditions .org/webextras
- clock or stopwatch
- pencils (one per table or team)
- plastic plates (one per table or team)

Directions

Ahead of time: Make white, orange, blue, and black ice cubes using food coloring. Make one color for each table. (To make orange mix yellow and red. To make black mix red and green.) Fill the cube trays up only halfway. If you make big cubes, they won't melt in time for this experiment.

During the program: Depending on your schedule and the weather, you can conduct this experiment outside.

- Lay out the four different colored ice cubes on a plastic plate.
- Keep time with the clock or stopwatch to see which melts first (black) and last (white).
- Allow time for the children to talk about what they find out.

Background Music
Sing-a-Long-Science by Warren Phillips (CDBY, 2008)

BOOKS TO DISPLAY

dePaola, Tomie. *Strega Nona.* Simon and Schuster, 1975.

Doudna, Kelly. *Super Simple Things to Do with Balloons.* Abdo, 2011. (This is one of many in the Super Simple Things to Do series.)

Moore, Eva. *Space Explorers.* Scholastic, 2000.

Shores, Lori. *How to Make a Liquid Rainbow.* Capstone, 2011. (This is one of many in the Hands-On Science Fun series.)

Weakland, Mark. *Gears Go, Wheels Roll.* Capstone, 2011. (This is one of many in the Science Starts series.)

Experiment Club (Grades 3–4)

Program Publicity

Help your child fine-tune teamwork skills at the XYZ Library. By conducting simple science experiments with others, children will learn about the world around them, have fun, expand their grasp of science concepts, and discover how to think for themselves. Balloons, homemade slime, and eggs will be some of their tools. Sign up at our website or call the library.

WEEK ONE

Reading Component (10 minutes)
Horrible Harry and the Green Slime by Suzy Kline (Puffin, 1998)
- Read pages 54–58, which describe Harry and Song Lee demonstrating how to make green slime.

Activity: Slime Making (15 minutes)
Supplies
- cornstarch (1 cup per child)
- water (½ cup per child)
- measuring cup (one per table)
- paper cups (one per child)
- food coloring
- sandwich-size plastic baggies (one per child)

Directions
- Have the children follow Harry's instructions and mix 1 cup of cornstarch and ½ cup of water and three drops of food coloring—then watch what happens.
- Let the children take their creations home in a plastic baggie.

Background Music
Here Comes Science by They Might Be Giants (Disney Sound, 2009)

WEEK TWO

Reading Component (10 minutes)
Hot Air: The (Mostly) True Story of the First Hot-Air Balloon Ride by Marjorie Priceman (Atheneum Books for Young Readers, 2005)

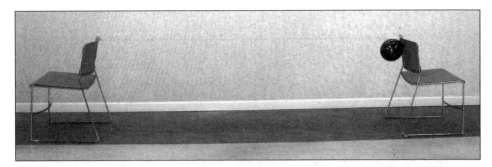

Figure 3.4 Balloon on chairs example

Activity: Flying Balloon Race (20 minutes)

Supplies
- balloon (one per child)
- string cut to 6-foot lengths (one per table)
- straws that do not have bendy tops (one per table)
- tape
- chairs (two per table)

Directions
- Make each table a team and ask each team to do the following:
- Place the chairs six feet apart (you can estimate).
- Thread the string through the straw.
- Tape the ends of the string to each chair, making sure the string is tight.
- Move the straws to the end of the string, closest to one chair. Make sure each team starts at the same side to create a race.
- Have one child from each team blow up one balloon. Have the child hold the balloon closed with his fingers (don't tie it!). Have another child tape one side of the balloon to the straw.
- Count to three and let the balloons go. Who wins?
- Allow time for each child on the team to compete against the other teams, blowing up their own balloons.

Background Music
Sid the Science Kid (Jim Henson Company, 2009)

WEEK THREE

Reading Component (10 minutes)
Humpty Dumpty Climbs Again by Dave Horowitz (Putnam, 2008)

Activity: Egg Roll Experiment (20 minutes)

The hard-boiled egg will spin longer because its center of gravity remains unchanged.

Supplies
- hard-boiled eggs labeled with an *H* (one per table)
- raw eggs labeled with an *R* (one per table)
- clock or stopwatch (one per table)
- pencil (one per table)
- paper (one per table)

Directions
- Have the children spin a hard-boiled egg and keep track of how long it spins using a clock or stopwatch. (They can also count how many times it spins.)
- Have the children spin a raw egg and keep track of how long it spins for using a clock or stopwatch. (They can also count how many times it spins.)
- Allow time for each child to have a turn at spinning the eggs, keeping track of the time on a piece of paper.
- Make sure you have enough time for the tables to share their data.

Background Music

Science by Teacher and the Rockbots (Power Arts Company, 2005)

WEEK FOUR

Reading Component (5 minutes)

The Chocolate Touch by Patrick Skene Catling (HarperCollins, 2006)
- Read chapter 1, where you learn how much John Midas loves chocolate.

Activity: Chocolate Melt Contest (25 minutes)

The tables using aluminum foil on their paper plates will have a faster melting speed than the plain paper plates. The sun's energy reflects off the foil, speeding up the melting process.

Supplies
- small chocolate chips (one bag each of white, milk, and dark)
- six small plates
- aluminum foil
- clock or stopwatch (one per table)
- piece of paper (one per table)
- pencil (one per table)

Directions

Ahead of time: Freeze a handful of each kind of chocolate chips. Wrap three paper plates in foil.

During the program: This experiment works best outside on a hot summer day. You can still conduct it inside, although the chocolate might not melt entirely. You can turn off the lights in half of the room to mimic the shade.

- Give each table a paper plate, aluminum covered or plain.
- Have each team choose a few frozen chips and a few room-temperature chips in each variety (white, milk, dark).
- Have each team with an aluminum foil–covered plate sit in one of three areas: a shaded area, a partially shaded area, and a full-sun area. Have each team with a plain paper plate sit in three separate areas as well.
- Using a clock or stopwatch, have the children determine how long it takes to melt each chip, keeping track using a pencil and piece of paper. Which team's chips melted fastest? Why?
- Hopefully you won't have the Chocolate Midas Touch happen after this experiment!

Background Music
Sing-a-Long-Science by Warren Phillips (CDBY, 2008)

BOOKS TO DISPLAY

Beck, Esther. *Cool Odor Decoders*. Abdo, 2007. (This is one of many in the Cool series.)

Brent, Lynnette. *Acids and Bases*. Crabtree, 2008. (This is one of many in the Why Chemistry Matters series.)

Catling, Patrick Skene. *The Chocolate Touch*. HarperCollins, 2006.

Enz, Tammy. *Build Your Own Car*. Capstone, 2011. (This is one of many in the Build It Yourself series.)

Hopwood, James. *Cool Distance Assistants*. Abdo, 2007. (This is one of many in the Cool series.)

Horowitz, Dave. *Humpty Dumpty Climbs Again*. Putnam, 2008.

Kline, Suzy. *Horrible Harry and the Green Slime*. Puffin, 1998.

Lockwood, Sophie. *Experiment with Heat*. Cherry Lake, 2011. (This is one of many in the Junior Scientists series.)

Offill, Jenny. *11 Experiments That Failed*. Schwartz and Wade, 2011.

Priceman, Marjorie. *Hot Air: The (Mostly) True Story of the First Hot-Air Balloon Ride*. Atheneum Books for Young Readers, 2005.

Science Club (Grades 5–6)

Program Publicity

Join the Science Club at the XYZ Library and compete in an exciting Smell-a-Thon and a Potato-Pickup Contest. Use basic science tools to help your team in competitions. Learn about books that make science fun. Sign up for the fun by calling the library or visiting our website, www.xyzlibrary.org.

WEEK ONE

Reading Component (5 minutes)

Stink and the World's Worst Super-Stinky Sneakers by Megan McDonald (Candlewick, 2008)

- Read chapter 1, where Stink goes on a smelly field trip.

Activity: Smell-a-Thon (25 minutes)

Supplies

- paper or plastic cups (about ten per table)
- aluminum foil
- pencils (one per table)
- smelly foods, spices, or herbs, such as lemons, limes, onions, garlic, vanilla, cinnamon, mint, cilantro, rosemary

Directions

- Give each table the same smelly foods or spices. Ask the children to place each smelly sample in a different cup.
- Have them cover the cups with aluminum foil and poke a small hole in the foil with a pencil.
- Once each table finishes, have the children go around to the different tables to have a Smell-a-Thon.
- Before the session ends, have them group each scent together. Can they place all lemons on one table, all onions on another?

Background Music

Here Comes Science by They Might Be Giants (Disney Sound, 2009)

WEEK TWO

Reading Component (15 minutes)

Jamie O'Rourke and the Big Potato by Tomie dePaola (Whitebird, 1992)

Activity: Potato Pickup (15 minutes)

Supplies
- potato (one per table)
- drinking straws (one per child)

Directions
- Tell the children that you want them to pick up the potato with one straw. Give them time to try it out in different ways.
- If no one figures out how to do it, have them hold their thumb over one end of the straw, then plunge the other end into the potato. They should then be able to lift the potato.

Background Music

Sid the Science Kid (Jim Henson Company, 2009)

WEEK THREE

Reading Component (5 minutes)

Touching Spirit Bear by Ben Mikaelsen (Harper Teen, 2005)
- Booktalk this story and tell the children to pretend they must survive in Alaska.

Activity: Water Filter (25 minutes)

The sand filters out mud particles and the brown color from the coffee.

Supplies
- transparent 16-ounce cups (four per table)
- craft sticks (four per table)
- sand (1 cup per table)
- coffee (1 cup per table)
- coffee filters (two per table)
- pencils (one per table)
- measuring cups (one per table)
- muddy water (1 cup per table)
- permanent markers (one per table)

Directions

Ahead of time: Brew coffee so it has time to cool down before the children get there. If you don't have a coffeepot at work, you can brew it at home and bring it in a container. Take two empty transparent cups and lay two craft sticks on the top of each cup.

Figure 3.5 Coffee and Muddy Water

During the program: Take two more cups. Punch a hole in the bottom of each with a pencil. Using a permanent marker, label one cup "Muddy Water" and the other cup "Coffee."
  – Place the labeled cups on top of the craft sticks.
  – Take a coffee filter and place it in the bottom of each labeled cup, making sure it covers the holes.
  – Place ½ cup of sand inside each coffee filter.
  – Pour 1 cup of muddy water in the "Muddy Water" cup.
  – Pour 1 cup of coffee in the "Coffee" cup.
  – After the labeled cups drain into the empty cups, examine the evidence.
  – Allow time for the tables to report their findings and talk about what happened.

Background Music
Science by Teacher and the Rockbots (Power Arts Company, 2005)

WEEK FOUR

Reading Component (5 minutes)
Project Mulberry by Linda Sue Park (Clarion, 2005)
  – Booktalk this story in which the main character has to conduct a science experiment.

Activity: Sink or Float (25 minutes)
The eyedropper floats because of the air stuck inside it. When you squeeze the bottle, more water is forced into the eyedropper, and it sinks. When you let the bottle go back to normal, the eyedropper rises because there is less pressure.

Supplies
  – empty 2-liter bottles of soda with caps; you can take off the wrappers (one per table)

- eyedroppers (one per table)
- water (enough to fill each 2-liter bottle)

Directions
- Have the children fill the bottles with water.
- Allow time for each child to get a turn.
- Have them take the eyedropper and fill it halfway with water from the bottle.
- Have them drop the eyedropper into the bottle with its top facing upward.
- Have them put the cap back on the bottle.
- Have them play with the bottle, squeezing it and letting it go. What happens?
- After everyone has had a chance, talk with the children about what they think is happening.

Figure 3.6
Dropper in bottle

Background Music
Sing-a-Long-Science by Warren Phillips (CDBY, 2008)

BOOKS TO DISPLAY

Calhoun, Yael. *Plant and Animal Science Fair Projects*. Enslow, 2010.

dePaola, Tomie. *Jamie O'Rourke and the Big Potato*. Whitebird, 1992.

Gardner, Robert. *Electricity and Magnetism Science Fair Projects*. Enslow, 2010. (This is one of many in the Science Fair Projects series.)

Goodstein, Madeline. *Plastics and Polymers Science Fair Projects*. Enslow, 2010.

McDonald, Megan. *Stink and the World's Worst Super-Stinky Sneakers*. Candlewick, 2008.

Mikaelsen, Ben. *Touching Spirit Bear*. Harper Teen, 2005.

Oxlade, Chris. *Experiments with Sound*. Heinemann, 2009. (This is one of many in the Do It Yourself series.)

Park, Linda Sue. *Project Mulberry*. Clarion, 2005. (Booktalk.)

Rybolt, Thomas, and Robert C. Mebane. *Environmental Science Fair Projects*. Enslow, 2010.

Walker, Pam, and Elaine Wood. *Eco System Science Fair Projects*. Enslow, 2010.

Woodford, Chris. *Experiments with Electricity and Magnetism*. Gareth Stevens, 2010. (This is one of many in the Cool Science series.)

Chapter 4

Humor

EVERYONE LOVES TO LAUGH. LAUGHTER IS SO IMPORTANT IN A CHILD'S development. Laughter enhances teamwork, promotes group bonding, eases anxiety, improves mood, and even boosts the immune system. You can help teach the children of your community while laughing together with silly stories and activities. Children will have a lot of fun with these crafts, activities, and games (and I know you will, too!).

Laugh Out Loud Club (Grades K–2)

Program Publicity
Explore the silly world of picture books at the XYZ Library. Listen to tales of dogs skateboarding, a child waking up as flat as a pancake, and cows typing letters to their farmer. Create harebrained crafts, sing ridiculous songs, and laugh out loud at the library. Sign up before the deadline on (date).

WEEK ONE

Reading Component (5 minutes)
Stanley's Wild Ride by Linda Bailey (Kids Can Press, 2008)
- – Stanley the dog and his friends escape their backyards and go on a wild ride through the neighborhood using a skateboard, a bike, a wagon, and a roller skate.

Activity: Stanley's Skateboard (25 minutes)

Supplies
- copies of figure 4.1 (one per child)
  Download full-size pattern from
  www.alaeditions.org/webextras
- crayons, colored pencils, or markers

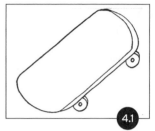

Directions
- Allow time for the children to decorate their
  own skateboards with crayons, colored pencils,
  or markers to have a wild time just like Stanley and his friends.

Music (3 minutes)

"Ride Ride Go for a Ride" by Buddy Castle, from *Balloons* (CD Baby, 2005)
- Practice starting, stopping, and turning left and right in this little ditty.

WEEK TWO

Reading Component (5 minutes)

Never Glue Your Friends to Chairs (Roscoe Riley series #1) by Katherine Applegate (HarperCollins, 2008)
- Read chapter 7, where Roscoe describes the bee antennae the class has to
  wear for parents' night for the big assembly.

Activity: Bee Antennae Headband (25 minutes)

Supplies
- chenille stems
- pom-poms
- strips of construction paper,
  2-by-12 inches (two per child)
- glue

Directions
- Have the children glue two strips
  of construction paper together to
  form a longer strip.
- Have them form the strip around
  their heads to create a headband,
  gluing the strips to fit.

Figure 4.2 Bee headband example

– Have them glue two chenille stems to the headband to resemble antennae.
– Have them glue a pom-pom on the tip of each chenille stem to complete their bumblebee headbands.

Music (3 minutes)
"Bumblebee" by Laurie Berkner, from *The Best of the Laurie Berkner Band* (Two Tomatoes, 2001)

WEEK THREE

Reading Component (5 minutes)
Click, Clack, Moo: Cows That Type by Doreen Cronin (Simon and Schuster, 2000)
– Cows go on strike from making milk because they want electric blankets to keep them warm at night.

Activity: Create Your Own Farmer Brown Story (25 minutes)
Supplies

– copies of figure 4.3 (one per child)
  Download full-size pattern from www.alaeditions .org/webextras
– pencils or pens
– crayons, colored pencils, or markers

Directions
– Children this age may not know what nouns and verbs are. Review with them: nouns are persons, places, or things; verbs are action words. If you have a whiteboard or an easel you can ask the children for suggestions of nouns and verbs and write them on the board so everyone can see. Pass out copies of figure 4.3 and ask the children to write down the farm animal, noun, and verb using crayon, colored pencil, or marker. Have them illustrate their silly story in the black box. Allow enough time so everyone can go around and read their story.

Music (3 minutes)
"Farmer Brown (Red Haired Boy)" by Leah Salomaa, from *I Like to Rise Family Folk Songs* (Girlfish Music, 2009)

WEEK FOUR

Reading Component (5 minutes)

Flat Stanley by Jeff Brown (Harper Trophy, 2003)
- Read chapter 1, which explains how Stanley becomes flat.

Activity: Flat Self (25 minutes)

Supplies
- copies of figure 4.4
  (one per boy)
- copies of figure 4.5
  (one per girl)
  *Download full-size patterns
  from www.alaeditions.org/
  webextras*
- crayons, colored pencils,
  or markers
- scissors (optional)

Directions
- Pass out copies of figures 4.4 and 4.5 to everyone. Instruct the children
  to create their own Flat Self. If time allows, you can have the children cut
  out their figures.

Music (4 minutes)

"Where in the World?" by the Brian Waite Band, from *Can't Sit Still* (CDBY,
  2007)
- Guess where in the world the singer is singing about.

BOOKS TO DISPLAY

Applegate, Katherine. *Never Glue Your Friends to Chairs*. HarperCollins, 2008.
  (This is one of many in the Roscoe Riley series.)

Bailey, Linda. *Stanley's Wild Ride*. Kids Can Press, 2010. (This is one of many in
  the Stanley series.)

Brown, Jeff. *Flat Stanley*. Harper Trophy, 2003. (This is one of many in the Flat
  Stanley series.)

Cronin, Doreen. *Click, Clack, Moo: Cows That Type*. Simon and Schuster, 2000.

McDonald, Megan. *Judy Moody*. Candlewick, 2010. (This is one of many in the
  Judy Moody series.)

McDonald, Megan. *Stink the Incredible Shrinking Kid*. Candlewick, 2006. (This is one of many in the Stink series.)

Pennypacker, Sara. *Clementine*. Hyperion, 2008. (This is one of many in the Clementine series.)

Willems, Mo. *Today I Will Fly!* Hyperion, 2007. (This is one of many in the Elephant and Piggie series.)

Roald Dahl Club (Grades 3–4)

Program Publicity

Roald Dahl is one of the most entertaining children's authors. His stories are laugh-out-loud funny and uniquely imaginative. Come to the XYZ Library to join the Roald Dahl Club. Listen to excerpts from his classic stories and create crafts and play games that accompany his books. Make a Pin the Tail on Mr. Fox game, a Peach-Rolling Flip Book, and a poster warning other children what witches really look like. Join the fun before it's too late! The deadline is (date)—you can sign up by calling the library or registering at the children's desk.

WEEK ONE

Reading Component (5 minutes)

James and the Giant Peach by Roald Dahl (Puffin, 2011)
   – Read chapter 16, where the peach rolls out of the garden, past a famous chocolate factory, and into the water.

Activity: Flip Book (25 minutes)

Supplies
   – copies of figure 4.6 (one per child)
   – copies of figure 4.7 (one per child)
      Download full-size patterns from www.alaeditions.org/ webextras

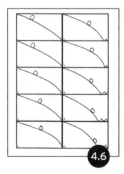
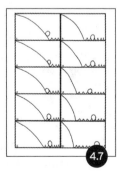

   – scissors (one pair per child or table)
   – stapler
   – crayons, colored pencils, or markers

Directions

 – Instruct the children to cut out the pages of the flip book. Have them place them in numerical order (the page numbers are in the lower left-hand corner), then place a staple on the left vertical side of the book. Have them color and add their own details (such as the house getting demolished). In order to make the flip book look as if it's moving, they have to draw the same thing but move it slightly on each page. When they flip it back and forth, the peach will look as if it's rolling up or down the hill.

Music (3 minutes)

"The Peach Rolls" by Randy Newman, from *James and the Giant Peach Soundtrack* (Walt Disney, 2002)

WEEK TWO

Reading Component (5 minutes)

Fantastic Mr. Fox by Roald Dahl (Puffin, 2007)

 – Read chapter 3, where Mr. Fox loses his tail.

Activity: Pin the Tail on Mr. Fox (25 minutes)

Supplies

 – copies of figure 4.8
 (one per child; you can either copy on colored paper, or provide crayons, colored pencils, or markers to decorate Mr. Fox)
 – copies of figure 4.9
 (one sheet makes six; one per child)
 Download full-size patterns from www.alaeditions.org/webextras
 – scissors
 – tape

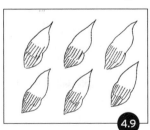

Directions

 – Have the children cut out Mr. Fox's tail.
 – Have them place a piece of tape to the back of the tail.
 – With their eyes closed, have them try to tape the tail on Mr. Fox.

– Allow time for each child to take turns at their table. To make the competition harder, have them spin around in a circle five times before playing.

Background Music
Fantastic Mr. Fox Soundtrack (Abkco, 2009)

WEEK THREE

Reading Component (10 minutes)
The Witches by Roald Dahl (Farrar, Straus and Giroux, 1983)
– Read chapter 3, where Grandma describes a witch: she has claws, she's bald, has big nose holes, eyes that change color, and no toes.

Activity: How to Recognize a Witch (15 minutes)

Supplies
– copies of figure 4.10 (one per table; you can copy on legal-size paper to create a poster)
  Download full-size pattern from www.alaeditions .org/webextras
– crayons, colored pencils, or markers

Directions
– After reading the passage aloud, tell the children that they need to make a warning poster for other children of how to recognize a witch. Have them either draw or write descriptions of what a witch looks like and what a witch does. Allow enough time for each table to present their poster to everyone.

Music (5 minutes)
"Pass the Broomstick" by Marcia Louis, from *Dancin' with Mr. Bones* (Marcia Louis, 2008)
– Use multiple rhythm sticks (or even pencils) for this hot potato game.

WEEK FOUR

Reading Component (10 minutes)

Charlie and the Chocolate Factory by Roald Dahl (Puffin, 2011)
- Read chapter 12, where Charlie brings home his winning ticket to tour the infamous and closely guarded chocolate factory.

Activity: Design Your Own Golden Ticket (15 minutes)

Supplies

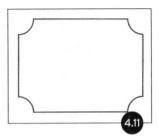

- copies of figure 4.11 on yellow paper, either computer paper or construction paper (one per child) *Download full-size pattern from www.alaeditions .org/webextras*
- crayons, colored pencils, or markers
- scissors (optional)

Directions
- Tell the children that there's a new contest . . . a golden ticket design contest. Using crayons, colored pencils, or markers, have them design their own golden ticket on yellow paper. (You may hand out scissors to cut the tickets out.) If time allows, have the children hold up their tickets and then vote for the winner.

Music (1 minute)

"Oompa Loompa" by Leslie Bricusse and Anthony Newley, from *Willy Wonka and the Chocolate Factory: Music from the Original Soundtrack* (Paramount, 1971)

BOOKS TO DISPLAY

Dahl, Roald. *The BFG.* Puffin, 2007.

Dahl, Roald. *Charlie and the Chocolate Factory.* Puffin, 2011.

Dahl, Roald. *Charlie and the Great Glass Elevator.* Puffin, 2007.

Dahl, Roald. *Danny, the Champion of the World.* Puffin, 2007.

Dahl, Roald. *The Enormous Crocodile.* Puffin, 2009.

Dahl, Roald. *Esio Trot.* Puffin, 2009.

Dahl, Roald. *Fantastic Mr. Fox*. Puffin, 2007.

Dahl, Roald. *George's Marvelous Medicine*. Puffin, 2007.

Dahl, Roald. *James and the Giant Peach*. Puffin, 2011.

Dahl, Roald. *The Magic Finger*. Puffin, 2009.

Dahl, Roald. *Matilda*. Puffin, 2007.

Dahl, Roald. *The Twits*. Puffin, 2009.

Dahl, Roald. *The Witches*. Farrar, Straus and Giroux, 1983.

Improv Club (Grades 5–6)

Program Publicity

Explore your creative side at the XYZ Library. Learn how to get up in front of an audience, think on your feet, and make people laugh. You'll play games such as Create an Infomercial, What's My Secret? and Name My Job. You'll listen to excerpts from books that make you laugh out loud, too! Join the Improv Club by the deadline—call the library or sign up at the children's desk.

WEEK ONE

Reading Component (5 minutes)
Cheesie Mack Is Not a Genius or Anything by Steve Cotler (Random House, 2011)
  – Read chapter 6 up to the point when Mack gets partially expelled for describing his principal, Mrs. Crespo.

Activity: The Secret Game (25 minutes)
Supplies
  – copy of figure 4.12
    *Download full-size pattern from www.alaeditions
    .org/webextras*

Directions
Ahead of time: Copy figure 4.12 and cut out the secrets. Fold them in half and put them in a cup.

During the program: Have the children pair up and pick a secret from the cup. Instruct them to act out a scene where two characters are discussing the secret

Secrets

I kept a library book forever.

My diary is under my mattress.

My family calls me Poopsie.

I still say I'm 9 when I go the movies so I can pay the kids' rate.

I ask for the bathroom pass when I don't really have to go.

There's a mouse living in my backpack.

I took my brother's favorite toy.

My favorite color is plaid.

I like the way crayons taste.

I lost my math book.

I made my mom a bracelet for her birthday.

I failed my spelling test.

There's a cat living in my tree house.

I'm wearing princess underwear.

I used scissors to cut a hole in my couch.

I still watch The Wiggles.

I broke my dad's favorite coffee mug.

I stole a pack of gum.

I can't add 2 + 2.

I don't know the ABC song.

I have a crush on my next-door neighbor.

I sleep with my blankie.

I still have training wheels on my bike.

I'm afraid of the dark.

I pierced my own ears.

My given name is Rumplestiltskin.

I don't have a middle name.

I eat paste.

I can't swim.

I'm ambidextrous.

without saying what the secret is. Give each pair one minute to act and have the "audience" guess the secret at the end of the minute.

Music

As Seen on TV (Game Show Theme Songs) by the Hit Crew (Turn Up the Music, 2007)

– Use the *Jeopardy* theme song while the audience thinks about their answers.

WEEK TWO

Reading Component (5 minutes)

How to Eat Fried Worms by Thomas Rockwell (Franklin Watts, 1973)
  – Read chapter 4, when Billy eats the first worm with ketchup, mustard, lemon, pepper, and horseradish.

Activity: Infomercial Game (25 minutes)

Supplies
  – copy of figure 4.13
    Download full-size pattern from www.alaeditions .org/webextras

Directions
Ahead of time: Copy figure 4.13 and cut out the product names. Fold them in half and put them in a cup.

Infomercial Products

Fried worms	Shoes that tie themselves
Shirt that folds itself	Book that reads aloud to you
Baseball-hitting bat	Flavor-changing juice
Crayon that stays in the lines	Self-combing comb
Pen that does math equations	Homework machine
Video game with infinite lives	Scissors that stay on the line
Bike that won't fall over	Color-changing pencil
Color-changing contact lenses	Cup that fills itself
Shoes that make you jump twenty feet high	Room-cleaning robot
Rocket pack	Tooth-brushing gum
Chocolate ants	Ant farm
Magic pillow	Invisible braces
Balloon with a prize inside	Sea monkeys
Soccer ball that stays in the air	Bike car
Pencil that spells correctly	Disappearing broccoli

During the program: Have each child take a turn and pick a product from the cup. Give each child a thirty-second time limit to "sell" the product to the group. At the end of the infomercial, request a show of hands to see how many children would buy the product. You can keep a tally to see what the most persuasive product is.

Music

As Seen on TV (Game Show Theme Songs) by the Hit Crew (Turn Up the Music, 2007)
   – Use the *Jeopardy* theme song while the audience thinks about their answers.

WEEK THREE

Reading Component (5 minutes)

Knucklehead: Tall Tales and Almost True Stories of Growing Up Scieszka by Jon Scieszka (Viking, 2008)
   – The children will enjoy listening to the short stories "Watch Your Brothers," and "Cooking" to highlight humor writing in this autobiographic book about growing up with five brothers.

Activity: Short Films (25 minutes)

Supplies
   – copy of figure 4.14
      Download full-size pattern from www.alaeditions .org/webextras

Directions
Ahead of time: Copy figure 4.14 and cut out movie title names. Fold them in half and put them in a cup.

During the program: Divide the children into groups of four. Have each group take a turn and pick a movie title from the cup. One child will be the narrator of the film, and the other three will be the actors. If you want to make the game more interesting, have the audience choose a genre such as horror, romance, or sci-fi for the actors to act out the short film. Give each group a two-minute time limit to perform. You can practice with three children as you read "Watch Your Brothers" for a second time while they perform the actions.

Movie Titles

The Giant Apple	Animals Loose
School Forever	School for the Gifted
The Toys	The Sewer Rats
The Museum	The Secret Book
The Science Experiment	The Car Key
The Magic Zoo	The Good Dad
The Time Cell Phone	The Wizard
The Triplets	The Yellow Ball
The Remote Control	The Garbage Pail Kids
The Red Box	Sharks
The Mean Witch	The Photo
The Endless Summer	The Baby
The Bicycle	The Video Game
Monsters under the Bed	Time Travelers
Green Slime	The Teddy Bear

Music

As Seen on TV (Game Show Theme Songs) by the Hit Crew (Turn Up the Music, 2007)
   – Use the *Jeopardy* theme song while the audience thinks about their answers.

WEEK FOUR

Reading Component (5 minutes)

Lawn Boy by Gary Paulsen (Wendy Lamb Books, 2007)
   – Read chapter 2, where Lawn Boy talks about his first day mowing lawns in order to make money for the summer.

Activity: What's Your Job? (25 minutes)

Supplies
- copy of figure 4.15

  Download full-size pattern from www.alaeditions.org/webextras

4.15

Directions

Ahead of time: Copy figure 4.15 and cut out the jobs. Fold them in half and put them in a cup.

During the program: Divide the children into groups of four and have each group take a turn and pick a product from the cup. Instruct the children that the four of them will pretend that they're at a friend's birthday party. Tell them to talk to their friends about their work. Make sure every child has time to talk. Give each group a two-minute time limit. At the end of the two minutes, have the audience guess their job.

Jobs

Zookeeper	Pilot
Lawyer	Television star
Police officer	Banker
Architect	EMT
Farmer	Dentist
Nurse	Dad
Reporter	Postal worker
Veterinarian	Artist
Dog walker	Coach
Lifeguard	Landscaper
Teacher	Librarian
Doctor	Movie star
Rock star	Professional athlete
Mechanic	Astronaut
Firefighter	Makeup artist

Music

As Seen on TV (Game Show Theme Songs) by the Hit Crew (Turn Up the Music, 2007)

Use the *Jeopardy* theme song while the audience thinks about their answers.

BOOKS TO DISPLAY

Atwater, Richard. *Mr. Popper's Penguins*. Little, Brown, 1988.

Bany-Winters, Lisa. *On Stage: Theatre Games and Activities for Kids*. Chicago Review Press, 1997.

Bany-Winters, Lisa. *Show Time! Music, Dance and Drama Activities for Kids*. Chicago Review Press, 2000.

Bedore, Bob. *101 Improv Games for Children and Adults*. Hunter House, 2004.

Blume, Judy. *Fudge-a-Mania*. Puffin, 2007.

Choldenko, Gennifer. *Al Capone Does My Shirts*. Perfection Learning, 2006.

Choldenko, Gennifer. *Al Capone Shines My Shoes*. Dial, 2009.

Cotler, Steve. *Cheesie Mack Is Not a Genius or Anything*. Random House, 2011.

Gantos, Jack. *Joey Pigza Swallowed the Key*. Square Fish, 2011. (This is one of many in the Joey Pigza series.)

Paulsen, Gary. *Lawn Boy*. Wendy Lamb Books, 2007.

Paulsen, Gary. *Lawn Boy Returns*. Yearling, 2011.

Rockwell, Thomas. *How to Eat Fried Worms*. Franklin Watts, 1973.

Rooyackers, Paul. *101 Drama Games for Children*. Hunter House, 1997.

Scieszka, Jon. *Knucklehead: Tall Tales and Almost True Stories of Growing Up Scieszka*. Viking, 2008.

Chapter 5

Art

MOST KIDS LIKE THE OPPORTUNITY TO EXPRESS THEMSELVES ARTISTICALLY. With budget cuts in public libraries and schools, they don't get the opportunity to do it enough. Give them a chance at your library. Purchase additional art supplies and let the children explore their artistic side. Using paint, tissue paper, and a variety of other mediums, they can become artists. Teach them about famous artists including Eric Carle, Jackson Pollack, and Georgia O'Keefe. Let the fun begin!

Masterpiece of the Week Club (Grades K–2)

Program Publicity

Let your creative juices flow while experimenting with drip painting and collage making in this after school program at XYZ Library. Listen to stories and learn about different types of art in the Masterpiece of the Week Club. Meetings will be held after school on (dates, times). For more information contact the XYZ Library.

WEEK ONE

Reading Component (5 minutes)

Art and Max by David Wiesner (Clarion, 2010)
- Two lizard friends, one an accomplished artist and the other a beginner, decide to paint together.

Activity: Drip Painting (25 minutes)

Supplies
- newspaper (enough to cover the tables with)
- 11-by-17-inch construction paper or posterboard (one per table)
- paper, plastic, or foam cups
- tempera paint in various colors
- cornstarch or glue to thicken paint

Directions
Ahead of time: Cover the tables with newspaper. Prepare the paint beforehand and thicken it with either cornstarch or glue. Poke one small hole in the bottom of one cup. Keep this cup inside another cup to keep the paint from dripping. Add about an inch of paint to the cup for the children to use. You can add more paint as needed.

During the program: Allow the children to drip paint in a Jackson Pollock style. Have them experiment by holding the drip cups at different heights from the paper.

Background Music
Lullaby Renditions of U2 (Rockabye Baby, 2007)

WEEK TWO

Reading Component (5 minutes)
Papa, Please Get the Moon for Me by Eric Carle (Simon and Schuster, 1991)
- A child begs her daddy to get the moon for her, and he gets a big ladder and climbs right up to it.

Activity: Tissue Paper Collage (25 minutes)
Supplies
- newspaper (enough to cover the tables with)
- sheets of tissue paper in assorted colors
- paints in assorted colors
- paintbrushes
- combs
- pencil erasers
- scissors

Directions

Ahead of time: Cover the tables with newspaper. Lay out sheets of tissue paper. Have volunteers use brushes, combs, and pencil erasers as paintbrushes, creating different textures in the paint just as Eric Carle does. Allow the paint to dry. Distribute a variety of tissue papers at each table.

During the program: When the paint dries, have the children cut the tissue paper into small squares to use to create a scene. They can cut out animals, grass, the moon, or even Papa!

Background Music
Lullaby Renditions of the Beatles (Rockabye Baby, 2007)

WEEK THREE

Reading Component (7 minutes)
The Hello, Goodbye Window by Norton Juster (Hyperion, 2005)
  – A child spends time at her grandparents' house, where the window is the center of the universe.

Activity: A Hello-Goodbye Window (25 minutes)
Supplies
  – white construction paper (one sheet per child)
  – crayons (preferably the thick kind you may have on hand for preschoolers)
  – strips of brown construction paper to create a window frame over the drawings (four per child)
  – glue

Directions
  – Have the children create their own Hello-Goodbye Window. Who would greet them? A parent, a pet, a friend?
  – Have them create that person using crayons on the white paper, pressing down hard with the crayons. Tell them they can be messy with their coloring to mimic the artist.
  – Have the children glue strips of brown construction paper over the drawing to create a window.

Background Music
Lullaby Renditions of the Rolling Stones (Rockabye Baby, 2007)

WEEK FOUR

Reading Component (5 minutes)

Ella Sarah Gets Dressed by Margaret Chodos-Irvine (Harcourt, 2003)
  – Ella Sarah wants to pick out her own outfits . . . even if they don't match.

Activity: Collage (25 minutes)

Supplies
  – magazines (you can use weeded ones, or ask each child to bring one in)
  – tissue paper
  – scrapbook paper
  – glue

Directions
  – Have the children draw a picture of Ella Sarah, or of themselves. Let the kids rip up pieces of magazines, tissue paper, and so on to create a collage effect. Have them glue the pieces onto their pictures to decorate their clothes.

Background Music

Lullaby Renditions of Led Zeppelin (Rockabye Baby, 2006)

BOOKS TO DISPLAY

Carle, Eric. *Papa, Please Get the Moon for Me.* Simon and Schuster, 1991.

Chodos-Irvine, Margaret. *Ella Sarah Gets Dressed.* Harcourt, 2003.

Degen, Bruce. *I Gotta Draw.* HarperCollins, 2012.

Intriago, Patricia. *Dot.* Farrar, Straus and Giroux, 2011.

Juster, Norton. *The Hello, Goodbye Window.* Hyperion, 2005.

Mayhew, James. *Katie Meets the Impressionists.* Scholastic, 2007. (This is one of many in the Katie series.)

Reynolds, Peter H. *The Dot.* Candlewick, 2003.

Saltzberg, Barney. *Beautiful Oops!* Workman Publishing, 2010.

Thomson, Bill. *Chalk.* Amazon Children's Publishing, 2010.

Tullet, Herve. *Press Here.* Chronicle Books, 2011.

Watt, Melanie. *Chester's Masterpiece.* Kids Can Press, 2010. (This is one of many in the Chester series.)

Wiesner, David. *Art and Max.* Clarion, 2010.

Caldecott Club (Grades 3–4)

Program Publicity
Do you want to become a picture book illustrator? Read award-winning books and learn how to experiment with art mediums to find your style. Create masterpieces using transparencies, scratchboard, and paper. Meetings will be held at the XYZ Library.

WEEK ONE

Reading Component (5 minutes)
Knuffle Bunny Too: A Case of Mistaken Identity by Mo Willems (Hyperion, 2007)
  – Two preschool girls mix up their favorite stuffed animals and realize their error in the middle of the night—much to their parent's misery.

Activity: Trixie at Your Library (25 minutes)
Supplies
  – photographs of your library (one for each child)
  – transparencies (copied with drawings of Trixie holding Knuffle Bunny)
  – paint or permanent markers
  – brads (four per child)

Directions
Ahead of time: Take a photo of your library. Blow it up to fit on an 8.5–by-11-inch piece of paper. Make black-and-white copies. Draw a sketch of Trixie and use a black-and-white copy machine to create Trixie transparencies. Line up a transparency with a photo of your library. Punch holes in each corner and place a brad in each hole.

During the program: Have the children paint or color (using permanent markers) Trixie in front of the library. This masterpiece will look like a piece of artwork from Willem's book.

Background Music
Lullaby Renditions of Metallica (Rockabye Baby, 2006)

WEEK TWO

Reading Component (5 minutes)

Flotsam by David Wiesner (Clarion, 2006)
- A boy finds an underwater camera that other children around the world have also discovered.

Activity: Self-Portrait (25 minutes)

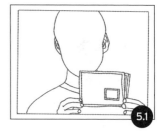

Supplies
- copies of figure 5.1 (one per child)
  Download full-size pattern from www.alaeditions.org/webextras
- crayons, colored pencils, or markers
- mirrors (one per table)

Directions

Let the kids create a self-portrait to make it look like they found the Flotsam camera. Have them draw their friends in the pictures within pictures.

Background Music

Lullaby Renditions of Nirvana (Rockabye Baby, 2006)

WEEK THREE

Reading Component (5 minutes)

The House in the Night by Susan Marie Swanson (Houghton Mifflin, 2008)
- A girl is given a gold key to a house that she makes her home by naming all the things inside of it.

Activity: Make Your Own Scratchboard (optional; 25 minutes, plus overnight dry time)

Use this as an additional activity before the next one, "Scratching Out Your House in the Night." If you don't have the budget to purchase scratchboards from a craft store, you can also use these directions for volunteers to make scratchboards ahead of time for the "Scratching Out Your House in the Night" activity.

Supplies
- cardstock or construction paper
- black tempera paint
- dishwashing detergent to add to black paint
- paintbrushes or foam brushes
- crayons (preferably the thick kind you may have on hand for preschoolers)

Directions
- Color designs using different colored crayons on the cardstock or construction paper. If you want to be authentic to *The House in the Night,* you can use only white and yellow crayons. Cover the entire sheet of paper with crayon.
- Add a few drops of dishwashing detergent to the black paint (this will make it easier for the paint to come off when scratched). Paint a thick layer on top of the crayon, covering completely, and let dry overnight.

Activity: Scratching Out Your House in the Night (25 minutes)

Use this as an activity if you purchase your own scratchboards, or once you've used the activity above at a separate club meeting *or as a volunteer preparation.*

Supplies
- scratchboards (one per child)
- bamboo skewers (to scratch paint off)

Directions
- Have the children use bamboo skewers to scratch paint off and make designs.

Background Music

Lullaby Renditions of Pink Floyd (Rockabye Baby, 2006)

WEEK FOUR

Reading Component (5 minutes)

Color Zoo by Lois Ehlert (HarperCollins, 1989)
- Turn the pages to see how different shapes create a variety of animals.

Activity: Color Zoo Mini Book (25 minutes)

Supplies
- copies of figure 5.2 on purple paper
  (each sheet makes two crafts; one craft per child)
- copies of figure 5.3 on blue paper
  (each sheet makes two crafts; one craft per child)
- copies of figure 5.4 on orange paper
  (each sheet makes two crafts; one craft per child)
- copies of figure 5.5 on white paper
  (each sheet makes two crafts; one craft per child)
  Download full-size patterns from www.alaeditions.org/webextras
- white paper for booklet (three sheets per child)
- scissors
- stapler
- glue or tape
- crayons, colored pencils, or markers

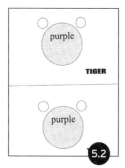 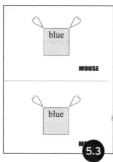 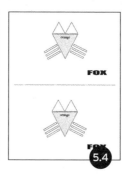 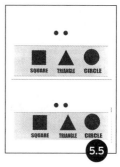

Directions

Ahead of time: Make copies on colored paper, then cut them in half on the horizontal line. Cut out the gray-shaded shapes on the Color Zoo copies (circle on tiger, square on mouse, triangle on fox). This part is a little tricky—I would highly recommend using volunteers to do this part of the cutting. Create a six-page booklet by folding three sheets of paper together and stapling.

During the program: Have the children glue or tape the Color Zoo animals to the inside pages of the booklet. Encourage the children to also come up with their own creatures using the basic shapes. Allow time for them to draw a cover for their booklet.

Background Music

Lullaby Renditions of the Dave Matthews Band by Sleepytime Tunes (Copycats, 2009)

BOOKS TO DISPLAY

Crews, David. *Truck*. Greenwillow Books, 1981.

Ehlert, Lois. *Color Zoo*. HarperCollins, 1989.

Fleming, Denise. *In the Small, Small Pond*. Holt, 1994.

Henkes, Kevin. *Kitten's First Full Moon*. Greenwillow Books, 2005.

Macaulay, David. *Black and White*. Houghton, 1991.

Pinkney, Jerry. *The Lion and the Mouse*. Little, Brown, 2010.

Priceman, Marjorie. *Hot Air: The (Mostly) True Story of the First Hot Air Balloon Ride*. Anne Schwartz, 2006.

Raschka, Chris. *A Ball for Daisy*. Schwartz and Wade, 2012.

Rylant, Cynthia. *The Relatives Came*. Bradbury, 1986.

Seeger, Laura Vaccaro. *First the Egg*. Roaring Brook, 2008.

Sendak, Maurice. *Where the Wild Things Are*. Harper, 1964.

Swanson, Susan Marie. *The House in the Night*. Houghton Mifflin, 2008.

Wiesner, David. *Flotsam*. Clarion, 2006.

Willems, Mo. *Knuffle Bunny Too: A Case of Mistaken Identity*. Hyperion, 2007.

Artist of the Week Club (Grades 5–6)

Reading Component (5 minutes)

Chasing Vermeer by Blue Balliett (Scholastic, 2005)

– Booktalk *Chasing Vermeer*. Imagine solving a mystery: who stole a famous Vermeer painting? Help Petra and Calder in this interactive mystery where the clues are hidden in the illustrations.

Activity: Cezanne Still Life (Apples, Peaches, Pears and Grapes) (25 minutes)

Supplies

– paint
– basket
– sheet
– assorted fruit (apples, peaches, pears, and grapes)
– copies of figure 5.6 (optional; one per child)
  Download full-size pattern from www.alaeditions .org/webextras

Directions

Ahead of time: Set up a real-life still life in the middle of the room. Have supplies out ahead of time so the children will have enough time to paint.

During the program: Make sure children use thick black lines to outline everything like Cezanne did. If this is too much of an undertaking, provide copies of the Cezanne *Still Life* for everyone to paint on.

Background Music

Lullaby Renditions of Coldplay (Rockabye Baby, 2006)

WEEK TWO

Reading Component (5 minutes)

Red Blazer Girls: The Mistaken Masterpiece by Michael D. Beil (Knopf, 2011)
- Booktalk *Red Blazer Girls*. The four Blazer girls—Becca, Leigh Ann, Margaret, and Sophie—are recruited to help authenticate a painting. Mayhem and mystery follow them as they uncover the truth.

Activity: Georgia O'Keefe Flower (25 minutes)

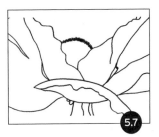

Supplies
- assorted flowers or poppies (you can ask a local floral shop to donate some; one per table) OR copies of figure 5.7 (one per child) *Download full-size pattern from www.alaeditions.org/webextras*
- paint
- paintbrushes
- construction paper to paint on

Directions
- You can either copy the Georgia O'Keefe flower for everyone or just have white paper for everyone to paint on. You can purchase six different flowers and place one on each table to use as a model when painting.

Background Music

Lullaby Renditions of Bob Marley (Rockabye Baby, 2007)

WEEK THREE

Reading Component (5 minutes)

Masterpiece by Elise Broach (Square Fish, 2010)
- Booktalk *Masterpiece*. An unlikely friendship between a boy and a beetle set the stage for this mystery. A famous drawing by artist Albrecht Durer is stolen at the Metropolitan Museum of Art, and James and Marvin help recover it.

Activity: Cubism Portrait (25 minutes)

Supplies
- paint
- paintbrushes
- construction paper to paint on
- copies of figure 5.8 (optional; one per child)
  Download full-size pattern from www.alaeditions .org/webextras

Directions
- You can copy Picasso's *Three Musicians* for everyone or supply white construction paper to paint on. Have the children create a cubist portrait.

Background Music

Lullaby Renditions of Pearl Jam (Rockabye Baby, 2010)

WEEK FOUR

Reading Component (5 minutes)

Mirrorscape by Mike Wilks (Egmont USA, 2010)
- Booktalk *Mirrorscape*. Mel Womper takes an art apprenticeship with a master painter. He's excited because he'll get to use color—an expensive pleasure in this dismal futuristic world.

Activity: Monet's Bridge at Giverny (25 minutes)

Supplies
- paint or pastels
- cotton swabs
- glitter or salt
- copies of figure 5.9 (optional; one per child)
  Download full-size pattern from www.alaeditions.org/webextras

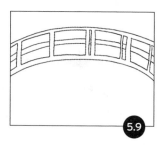

Directions
- Copy Monet's bridge at Giverny for everyone or supply white construction paper to paint on.
- If possible, you can take the kids outside to do this project. If you have trees and flowers, you can use those as inspiration. The children can use either paint or pastels. Have them use a variety of brushes or cotton

swabs to bring diversity in the strokes. Monet's paintings have an iridescent look to them—sprinkle glitter or salt into the paint to get a genuine look.

Background Music

Lullaby Renditions of Journey (Rockabye Baby, 2010)

BOOKS TO DISPLAY

Balliett, Blue. *Chasing Vermeer*. Scholastic, 2005.

Beil, Michael D. *Red Blazer Girls: The Mistaken Masterpiece*. Knopf, 2011.

Broach, Elise. *Masterpiece*. Square Fish, 2010.

Children's Illustrator series. Abdo, 2012.

D'Harcourt, Claire. *Art Up Close: From Ancient to Modern*. Chronicle, 2006.

D'Harcourt, Claire. *Louvre Up Close*. Chronicle, 2007.

D'Harcourt, Claire. *Masterpieces Up Close: Western Painting from the 14th to 20th Centuries*. Chronicle, 2006.

First Drawing series. Abdo, 2007.

Konigsburg, E. L. *From the Mixed-Up Files of Mrs. Basil E. Frankweiler*. Atheneum Books for Young Readers, 2007.

Mcmillan, Sue. *How to Improve at Drawing*. Crabtree, 2010.

Temple, Kathryn. *Art for Kids*. Lake Crafts, 2005.

Wilks, Mike. *Mirrorscape*. Egmont USA, 2010.

Mysteries

THERE ARE MANY MYSTERIES TO SOLVE IN THE LITERARY WORLD. AND WHO doesn't like to put on their detective hat every once in a while! Whether you're super sleuthing or CSI-ing, you'll enjoy teaching children about the mysteries of the world with these programs.

I Spy Club (Grades K–2)

Program Publicity

Use your detective eyes at the XYZ Library to spy things that begin with the letter *s* and men dressed in red-and-white stripes. In addition to spying Waldo, you'll learn to decode secret messages in the library's I Spy Club. Become a detective during the month of (month)! Register at the children's desk by (date).

WEEK ONE

Reading Component (5 minutes)

I Spy by Jean Marzollo (Scholastic, 1999)
– Have *I Spy* books out for the children to browse. If you have an overhead projector you can show all the children a spread to play the game as a group.

Activity: I Spy Game (25 minutes)

Supplies
- glue
- pencils
- construction paper
- Clean out your craft cabinet! All of those odds and ends you don't have enough of will be perfect for this activity. Pile an assortment of pom-poms, feathers, buttons, beads, stickers, and anything else you have around on the tables where the children will work.

Directions
- Instruct the children to create their own I Spy page. Using glue, attach craft supplies to the construction paper. Once they are finished gluing, have them use a pencil to write down clues for the I Spy challenge; for example, *I spy three blue pom-poms.* If time allows, shift everyone around and see if they can solve someone else's I Spy.

Music (5 minutes)

"Spy a Shape" by Dr. Jean, from *Totally Math* (Melody House, 2009)
- Find a circle, square, triangle, and rectangle in the room. Use your finger in the air to write the shapes as Dr. Jean instructs.

WEEK TWO

Reading Component (5 minutes)

Where's Waldo? by Martin Handford (Candlewick, 2007)
- Depending on the number of children you have, you can either open up a spread to search for Waldo as a group, or pass out different Waldo books for each table to search him out.

Activity: Where's Waldo? (25 minutes)

Supplies
- pencils, crayons, colored pencils, or markers (make sure you have red and white!)
- construction paper

Directions
- Create your own Where's Waldo puzzle. Begin by drawing Waldo in his striped costume. Fill the page with a busy scene. Don't forget to include lots of red-and-white-striped herrings!

Music (3 minutes)

"Can You Find the Color" by Abridge Club, from *Smart Moves 1: Tots Thru Pre-K* (Russ InVision, 2004)
  – After finding colors in the room, do different movement activities. For example: find yellow and move in slow motion, find white and jump, find blue and shake.

WEEK THREE

Reading Component (5 minutes)

The Big Bug Search by Caroline Young (Usborne Books, 2010)
  – If you have an overhead projector, use it to display the pages to the children. If not, pass the book around so everyone gets a chance to see it.

Activity: Create Your Own Search (25 minutes)

Supplies
  – magazines (either weeded library copies, or each child can bring some from home)
  – scissors
  – glue
  – construction paper

Directions
  – Let the children create their own search. It can be of animals, people, colors, places—anything they can think of. Their search can vary with the magazines that are available. If time allows, put some completed works on the overhead projector to search as a group.

Music (3 minutes)

"Can You Find the Color" by Abridge Club, from *Smart Moves 2: Preschool Thru 1st* (Russ InVision, 2004)
  – After finding shapes in the room, do different movement activities. For example: find a square and hop.

WEEK FOUR

Reading Component (10 minutes)
The Mystery of King Karfu by Doug Cushman (HarperCollins, 1998)

Activity: Decode the Secret (15 minutes)
Supplies
- copies of "Key to the Secret Code" (one per child)
- copies of the two secret codes in the story (one of each per child)
- pencils

Directions
- Distribute copies of the "Key to the Secret Code" and the two secret codes hidden in the story to each child. Allow time for the children to solve the mysteries. The answer to the first code is: "Go to the King's chamber, turn left, open third door, lift fourth stone on floor." The answer to the second code is: "In the name of Isis, take the mashed grape, and spread it on bread, take the mashed peanut, and spread on bread, fold it over and eat."

Music (4 minutes)
"Peanut Butter and Jelly" by Greg and Steve, from *Fun and Games* (Greg and Steve Productions, 2002)
- Celebrate breaking the code and dance to the sandwich song!

BOOKS TO DISPLAY

Clement, Rod. *Grandpa's Teeth*. HarperCollins, 1998.

Cushman, Doug. *The Mystery of King Karfu*. HarperCollins, 1998.

Handford, Martin. *Where's Waldo?* Candlewick, 2007. (This is one of many in the Waldo series.)

Kellogg, Steven. *The Missing Mitten Mystery*. Puffin, 2002.

Marzollo, Jean. *I Spy*. Scholastic, 1999. (This is one of many in the I Spy series.)

Palatini, Margie. *Bad Boys*. Katherine Tegen Books, 2006. (This is one of many in the Bad Boys series.)

Teague, Mark. *Detective LaRue*. Scholastic, 2004.

Wiesner, David. *Tuesday*. Clarion, 1991.

Young, Caroline. *The Big Bug Search*. Usborne Books, 2010.

Super Sleuth Club (Grades 3–4)

Contributed by Cheryl Thompson Cox, Children's Librarian, Springfield Town Library, Springfield, Vermont

Program Publicity

Calling all sleuths! Children in grades 3–4 are invited to hone their mystery-solving skills and become super sleuths at the library. This series book club will include activities that feature the mystery characters Jigsaw Jones, Encyclopedia Brown, Chet Gecko, and the A-Z Mysteries Gang. Learn how to create invisible inks, how to identify fingerprints, and how to decode a variety of ciphers through the four-week program.

WEEK ONE

Reading Component (5 minutes)

The Case of the Detective in Disguise by James Preller (Scholastic, 2001)
- Read chapter 4, "The Missing Brownies," and ask for predictions. Discuss Jigsaw's techniques (wearing a disguise and writing in code) and how those techniques could help catch the thief.

Activity: St. Cyr Slide Code (25 minutes)

Supplies
- copies of figure 6.1
  (one sheet makes four crafts; one craft per child)
- copies of figure 6.2
  (one per child)
  Download full-size patterns from www.alaeditions.org/ webextras
- scissors
- pencils
- scrap paper

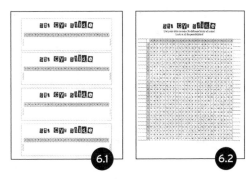

Directions
Cut out the St. Cyr slide (figure 6.1) for each child.
- Have the children make two slits (under the A and Z).
- Have them cut out the slide codes (figure 6.2) horizontally.

- Have the children decide on a code to use and weave it through the slits, then writing a secret message. For example, if they use the Z code to write "This is so cool," the code would be "Sghr hr rn bnnk."
- Ask the children to trade messages to see if their partner can solve the secret.

Music (5 minutes)

Use a beanbag or a ball to be the cookie. Sing the popular chant to dismiss the children until next week.

> *Who Stole the Cookie from the Cookie Jar?*
>
> Who stole the cookie from the cookie jar?
>
> (Name) stole the cookie from the cookie jar!
>
> Who, me?
>
> Yes, you.
>
> Couldn't be.
>
> Then who?

Repeat until each child has been chosen.

WEEK TWO

Reading Component (5 minutes)

Encyclopedia Brown and the Case of the Treasure Hunt by Donald J. Sobol (Yearling, 1989)
- Read chapter 4 and ask the kids to solve the case.

Activity: Caesar Cipher Secret Decoder (25 minutes)

Supplies
- copies of figure 6.3 (each sheet makes four crafts; one craft per child)
- copies of figure 6.4 (each sheet makes two crafts; one craft per child)
  Download full-size pattern from www.alaeditions.org/ webextras

 6.3

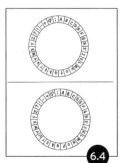 6.4

– scissors
– brads (one per child)

Directions
- Have children cut out both circles and fasten them together with a brad.
- Have each child decide on a code and write a secret message; for example, letting L = ♥, "Fb♥i!az vbwxf !f yha" would be "Solving codes is fun."
- Ask them to trade messages and see if their partner can solve the secret.

Music (5 minutes)
Use a beanbag or a ball to be the cookie. Sing the popular chant to dismiss the children until next week.

> *Who Stole the Cookie from the Cookie Jar?*
>
> Who stole the cookie from the cookie jar?
>
> (Name) stole the cookie from the cookie jar!
>
> Who, me?
>
> Yes, you.
>
> Couldn't be.
>
> Then who?

Repeat until each child has been chosen.

WEEK THREE

Reading Component (5 minutes)
The Orange Outlaw by Ron Roy (Random House, 2001)
- Read chapter 3 and ask the kids to predict what will happen.

Activity: Fingerprinting (25 minutes)
Supplies
- copies of figure 6.5 (one per child)
  Download full-size pattern from www.alaeditions.org/webextras
- pencils
- white copy paper
- transparent tape

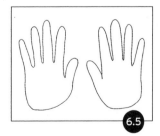
6.5

Directions
- Have the children rub a small dark area with the pencil on a sheet of white copy paper.
- Have them press and rub one finger in the pencil-lead dust.
- Have them place the sticky side of a piece of transparent tape on top of the lead-covered finger.
- Have them pull the tape off the finger and adhere it to the corresponding finger on figure 6.5.
- Continue until each child has all ten fingers printed.
- If time allows, discuss fingerprint arches, loops, and whorls and let the children figure out which patterns they have. Use *Whose Fingerprints Are These? Crime-Solving Science Projects* by Robert Gardner (Enslow, 2010) as a reference.

Music (5 minutes)
Use a beanbag or a ball to be the cookie. Sing the popular chant to dismiss the children until next week.

> *Who Stole the Cookie from the Cookie Jar?*
> Who stole the cookie from the cookie jar?
> (Name) stole the cookie from the cookie jar!
> Who, me?
> Yes, you.
> Couldn't be.
> Then who?

Repeat until each child has been chosen.

WEEK FOUR

Reading Component (10 minutes)
The Malted Falcon by Bruce Hale (Harcourt, 2003)
- Read pages xi-xiii and chapter 6. Who do the kids think will get to eat the Malted Falcon?

Activity: Invisible Ink (15 minutes)
These ingredients will produce five different recipes for invisible ink. If your budget is tight, just make one. If possible, create a few different ones to exper-

iment with and see which works best. You can have the children create secret messages and then pass them around to reveal what the note says.

Supplies
- cotton swabs (box of one hundred)
- white copy paper (two sheets per child)
- cups
- lemon juice (1 ounce per table)
- lime juice (1 ounce per table)
- orange juice (1 ounce per table)
- apple juice (1 ounce per table)
- salt to pour
- crayons
- measuring cup
- baking soda (¼ cup per table)
- water (½ cup per table)
- grape juice (purple, not green or white; 4 ounces per table)

Directions

Invisible Ink using Acidic Fruit Juices
- Place four cups on the table. Pour about an inch of juice in each cup: create one lemon juice, one lime juice, one orange juice, and one apple juice. Place one cotton swab in each cup, creating four "pens."
- Have the children use this "pen" to write a secret message on white copy paper.
- Have them pour salt on the juice while it's still wet.
- Let the juice dry completely.
- Have the children brush off the salt.
- Have them use a crayon to color in the page and reveal their secret messages.

Invisible Ink Using Baking Soda
- Using a measuring cup, pour ¼ cup of baking soda and ½ cup of water into a cup.
- Have the children use a cotton swab as a "pen" to dip in the mixture and write a message on white copy paper.
- Let the mixture dry completely.
- Have the children use a cotton swab and dip it into the grape juice, painting the page to reveal their secret messages.

Music (5 minutes)

Use a beanbag or a ball to be the cookie. Sing the popular chant to dismiss the children until next week.

> *Who Stole the Cookie from the Cookie Jar?*
>
> Who stole the cookie from the cookie jar?
>
> (Name) stole the cookie from the cookie jar!
>
> Who, me?
>
> Yes, you.
>
> Couldn't be.
>
> Then who?

Repeat until each child has been chosen.

BOOKS TO DISPLAY

Base, Graeme. *The Eleventh Hour*. Puffin, 1997.

Hale, Bruce. *The Malted Falcon*. Harcourt, 2003. (This is one of many in the Chet Gecko series.)

Kitamura, Satoshi. *Sheep in Wolves' Clothing*. Andersen Press, 2009.

Macaulay, David. *Black and White*. Sandpiper, 2005.

Preller, James. *The Case of the Detective in Disguise*. Scholastic, 2001. (This is one of many in the Jigsaw Jones series.)

Roy, Ron. *The Orange Outlaw*. Random House, 2001. (This is one of many in the A to Z Mysteries series.)

Sobol, Donald J. *Encyclopedia Brown and the Case of the Treasure Hunt*. Yearling, 1989. (This is one of many in the Encyclopedia Brown series.)

Sobol, Donald J. *Two-Minute Mysteries*. Scholastic, 1991.

Van Allsburg, Chris. *The Mysteries of Harris Burdick*. Houghton, 1984.

CSI Club (Grades 5–6)

Program Publicity
Do you think that you have what it takes to become a crime scene investigator? Learn how to take shoe impressions and fingerprints, and how to analyze handwriting. Put it all together at the end of the month to solve a murder in the XYZ Library. To get your assignment, visit the library by (date).

WEEK ONE

Reading Component (5 minutes)
Stormbreaker by Anthony Horowitz (Puffin, 2000)
  - Read chapter 1, when Alex learns of his Uncle Ian's death and his mysterious life.

Activity: Shoe Impressions (25 minutes)
Supplies
  - copies of figure 6.6 on legal-size paper to accommodate foot size (one per child)
  - copies of figure 6.7 (one per child)
    Download full-size patterns from www.alaeditions.org/ webextras
  - crayons

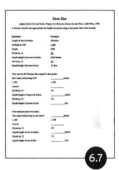

Directions
  - Have each child place their shoe against the back side of figure 6.6.
  - Take the side of a crayon and rub it along the front side of the paper to create a shoe impression.
  - Ask the children to pass their shoe impressions to you. Mix them up and hand them back. See if the children can figure out whose shoe they have by using the formula from figure 6.7.

Background Music
The Ultimate James Bond Collection by City of Prague Philharmonic Orchestra (Edel, 2007)

WEEK TWO

Reading Component (5 minutes)
Double or Die by Charlie Higson (Hyperion Books for Children, 2007)
- Read parts of chapter 2, pages 19–25, beginning with "What's a cipher?"

Activity: Handwriting Analysis (25 minutes)

Supplies
- copies of figure 6.8 (one per child)
- pens
- tracing paper (one sheet per child)
  *Download full-size pattern from www.alaeditions
  .org/webextras*

Directions
- Ask the children to fill out the London Letter form. Ask them to write their names on the backs of the sheets.
- Have them take a sheet of tracing paper and place it on top of the London Letter.
- Have them use dots to mark the tops of letters such as *f* and *t* and the bottoms of letters such as *y* and *g*.
- Have them connect the dots to create lines. The angle of someone's handwriting is unique.
- Mix up the tracing paper and London Letters by table. Redistribute and see if the children can guess whose writing is whose by matching the angles of the handwriting.

Background Music
Ultimate Pink Panther by Henry Mancini (BMG Music, 2004)

WEEK THREE

Reading Component (5 minutes)
Framed! by Malcolm Rose (Kingfisher, 2005)
- Read chapter 3, where Luke is assessing a "murder" in his Year 10 class as a forensic investigator.

Activity: Fingerprint Analysis (25 minutes)

Supplies
- copies of figure 6.9 (one per child)
- copies of figure 6.10 (one per child)
  Download full-size patterns from www.alaeditions.org/webextras
- pencils
- white copy paper
- transparent tape
- washable black ink (optional)

Directions
- Have the children rub a small dark area with the pencil on a sheet of white copy paper.
- Have them press and rub one finger in the pencil-lead dust.
- Have them place the sticky side of a piece of transparent tape on top of the lead-covered finger.
- Have them pull the tape off and adhere it to the corresponding finger on figure 6.9.
- Continue until each child has all ten fingers "printed."
- If your budget allows, you can fingerprint the children with washable black ink instead of using pencil lead.
- After everyone is fingerprinted, let the children figure out what ridgeline patterns and details they have in their fingerprints using figure 6.10 as a guide.

Background Music
The Thomas Crown Affair Soundtrack by Bill Conti (Ark 21, 1999)

WEEK FOUR

Reading Component (5 minutes)
The London Eye Mystery by Siobhan Dowd (David Fickling Books, 2008)
- Read chapter 7, where Salim disappears at the Ferris wheel while Ted and Kat are talking.

Activity: Solve the Murder (25 minutes)

Supplies

- copy of figure 6.11
- four copies of figures 6.12 (one for you, one for the judge, one for the lawyer, and one for the suspects)
- four copies of 6.13
- four copies of figure 6.14
- four copies of figure 6.15
- four copies of figure 6.16
- copies of figure 6.17 (one per jury member)
- two copies of figure 6.18
- four copies of figure 6.6 (above)
  Download full-size patterns from www.alaeditions.org/webextras
- pencils for jury members to take notes
- three manila folders or envelopes
- box labeled "At the Scene of the Crime" (you can use a small book box or shoe box)
- crayons
- clothes to use to get the children in character (optional; you can use a mallet and a graduation robe for the judge, and a shirt and tie for the lawyer)

6.11

6.12

6.13

6.14

6.15

6.16

6.17

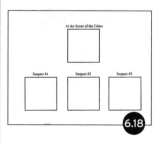
6.18

Directions

Ahead of time: Cut up the cells from figure 6.11 and place them in a cup. (You need to make sure you have at least five children to do this activity. You can play the role of the lawyer if needed.)

Set up the room with a table in front to seat the judge and suspect. Have the jury members sit on the floor or in chairs facing the table. Have tables in the back of the room so jurors can have room and space to work on the clues.

During the program: As the children walk through the door, you can let them choose their role from the cup. Once everyone has a role, take the three suspects out of the room along with one copy of figure 6.6, two copies of figure 6.18, three manila folders or envelopes, one pencil, and one crayon. Label each envelope, one with *A*, one with *B*, and one with *C*.

Label one copy of figure 6.18 "Evidence A." Take Suspect 3's index fingerprint (using pencil lead) and place it in the box labeled "At the Scene of the Crime."

Label the copy of figure 6.6 "Evidence B." Take Suspect 1's shoe impression using the side of a crayon.

Label the other copy of figure 6.18 "Evidence C." Take Suspect 2's handwriting sample in the box labeled "At the Scene of the Crime." Have him write down "Crime and Detection, Traces, Crime Scene Science Fair Projects."

Put the corresponding evidence in each manila folder or envelope.

Return to the courtroom with the suspects and have them line up in front near the table. (If you'd rather, you can do this ahead of time using staff's fingerprints, etc. If time allows, it's more fun for the kids to figure this out on their own! You can have a child read *The London Eye Mystery* excerpt while you are setting up with the suspects.)

Read through each page of the script separately and give the children time to take each suspect's fingerprints, shoe impressions, and handwriting samples in between. You can use music as a time limit: give them the length of one or two songs to collect evidence and decide which suspect is guilty.

When you get to the end of the script, allow the jurors to decide which suspect is guilty. You can use this script over and over because the ending is based on the jurors' decision. How each suspect reads his role and answers the questions can make the jury decide one way or another.

Background Music

The Italian Job Soundtrack by John Powell (Varese Sarabande, 2003)

BOOKS TO DISPLAY

Berlin, Eric. *The Puzzling World of Winston Breen*. Puffin, 2009. (This is one of many in the Winston Breen series.)

Cooney, Caroline B. *The Face on the Milk Carton*. Bantam Doubleday, 1990.

Dowd, Siobhan. *The London Eye Mystery*. David Fickling Books, 2008.

Gaiman, Neil. *The Graveyard Book*. HarperCollins, 2008.

Higson, Charlie. *Double or Die*. Hyperion Books for Children, 2007. (This is one of many in the Young Bond series.)

Horowitz, Anthony. *Stormbreaker*. Puffin, 2000. (This is one of many in the Alex Rider series.)

Konigburg, E. L. *From the Mixed-Up Files of Mrs. Basil E. Frankweiler*. Atheneum, 2007.

Raskin, Ellen. *The Westing Game*. Dutton, 2003.

Rose, Malcolm. *Framed*. Kingfisher, 2005. (This is one of many in the Traces series.)

Snicket, Lemony. *The Bad Beginning*. HarperCollins, 1999. (This is one of many in the Series of Unfortunate Events series.)

Stead, Rebecca. *When You Reach Me*. Random House, 2009.

Chapter 7

Out at Sea

WHAT BETTER WAY TO SPEND A SUMMER MONTH THAN ON THE WATER?
Explore the world of pirates and Percy Jackson. Whether it be Jack Sparrow or
Poseidon, the children in your community will want to yell, "Yo, ho, ho!" when
they join your after school clubs.

Jolly Roger Club (Grades K–2)

Program Publicity

Pirates, and parrots, and treasure, oh my! Take a cruise at the XYZ Library and
listen to stories about mates. Create a Jolly Roger flag, pirate puppets for every
finger, and a pirate hat. Join the fun (dates and times).

WEEK ONE

Reading Component (5 minutes)
This Little Pirate by Philomen Sturges (Puffin, 2007)
  – Count to ten with this funny story about two sets of pirates who both
    want the treasure box.

Activity: Pirate Finger Puppets (25 minutes)

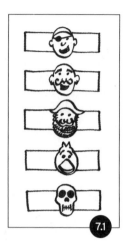

Supplies
- copies of figure 7.1 (one per child)
  Download full-size pattern from www.alaeditions.org/webextras
- crayons, colored pencils, or markers
- scissors
- glue or tape

Directions
- Have the children color the five pirate finger puppets using crayons, colored pencils, or markers.
- Have them use scissors cut out the puppets, and glue or tape to fit each puppet to their fingers.

Music (5 minutes)

"Ten Jolly Pirates" by Kidzone, from *Pirate Island* (Kidzone, 2010)
- Count down from ten with this pirate song.

WEEK TWO

Reading Component (5 minutes)

Roger, the Jolly Pirate by Brett Helquist (HarperCollins, 2007)
- Find out why the pirate flag is called the "Jolly Roger."

Activity: Jolly Roger Flag (25 minutes)

Supplies
- copies of figure 7.2 on cardstock (one per child)
  Download full-size pattern from www.alaeditions.org/webextras
- crayons, colored pencils, or markers

Directions
- Have the children decorate their flags using crayons, colored pencils, or markers. Have them create a different back story for the flag, just like the story of Jolly Roger.

Music (3 minutes)

"Jolly Old Roger" by Sam Hinton, from *Whoever Shall Have Some Peanuts*
(Folkways Records, 1964)
- Clap or sway along to the song about good ol' Jolly Roger.

WEEK THREE

Reading Component (5 minutes)

How I Became a Pirate by Melinda Long (Harcourt, 2003)
- Jeremy Jacob is building a sand castle on the beach when a pirate ship
  invites him aboard.

Activity: Pirate Hat (25 minutes)

Supplies
- copies of figure 7.3 on cardstock
  (one per child)
  *Download full-size pattern from
  www.alaeditions.org/webextras*
- crayons, colored pencils, or markers
- glue or tape

Directions
- Have the children decorate the pirate hat using crayons, colored pencils,
  or markers.
- Have them cut out the pirate hat and the extra strips below it.
- Have them glue or tape the strips of paper to fit their head, and then glue
  or tape the pirate hat to the headband.

Music (3 minutes)

"Row Your Boat" by Gotta Crow, from *Mother Goose Rocks Volume 4* (Lightyear, 2002)
- Join the festivities with this Sheryl Crow–esque sing-along as you parade
  around with your new hat.

WEEK FOUR

Reading Component (5 minutes)

I Love My Pirate Papa by Laura Leuck (Harcourt, 2007)
- This sweet bedtime story describes how much a little boy's daddy loves him.

Activity: Pirate Bracelet (25 minutes)

Supplies
- chenille stems (one per child)
- pony beads (a one-pound bag of assorted colors; about 40 per child)
- skull beads
- paper cups or plates (optional)

Directions
- Have the children thread the pony beads and skull beads on the chenille stem to create a pirate bracelet. (You may find it easier to place pony beads in paper cups or plates at each table so the beads don't roll off the tables.) Suggest that the children create a pattern.
- When the children are finished beading, have them place the stem around the wrist and twist the ends together to make a bracelet.

Music (3 minutes)

"Day-O (Banana Boat)" by Harry Belafonte, from *Very Best of Harry Belafonte* (RCA, 2001)
- Let the children dance around to this silly song, showing off their new bracelets.

BOOKS TO DISPLAY

Courtauld, Sarah. *On a Pirate Ship*. Usborne, 2007.

Duddle, Jonny. *The Pirate Cruncher*. Templar, 2010.

Harris, Peter. *Night Pirates*. Scholastic, 2006.

Helquist, Brett. *Roger, the Jolly Pirate*. HarperCollins, 2007.

Kramer, Andrew. *Pajama Pirates*. HarperCollins, 2010.

Leuck, Laura. *I Love My Pirate Papa*. Harcourt, 2007.

Long, Melinda. *How I Became a Pirate*. Harcourt, 2003.

Long, Melinda. *Pirates Don't Change Diapers*. Harcourt, 2007.

Sturges, Philomen. *This Little Pirate*. Puffin, 2007.

Pirates Club (Grades 3–4)

Program Publicity
Come to the XYZ Library and join the Pirate Club to go to Pirate School. Learn how to create your own desert island, a paper ship that actually floats, and knots to keep your boat at the dock. For more information contact the children's desk. Use the code phrase: Yo ho ho!

WEEK ONE

Reading Component (5 minutes)
The Curse of Snake Island by Brian James (Grosset and Dunlap, 2007)
  - Read chapter 6, when Pete and his pirate-in-training friends land on Snake Island.

Activity: Design Your Own Deserted Island (25 minutes)
Supplies
  - posterboard or construction paper
  - crayons, colored pencils, or markers

Directions
  - Give each child a piece of posterboard or construction paper so they can design their own deserted island. They can create an island in any shape, and it could have an *X* to mark buried treasure, a campsite, and anything else their imaginations come up with.

Background Music
Island Songs for Children by David Kirton (Bird's Eye Music, 2011)

WEEK TWO

Reading Component (5 minutes)
The Tale of Billy Turner and Other Stories by Rob Kidd (Disney Press, 2009)
  - Read the short story "The Cat's Meow."

Activity: Wanted Poster (25 minutes)

Supplies
- copies of figure 7.4 (one per child)
  Download full-size pattern from www.alaeditions.org/webextras
- crayons, colored pencils, or markers

Directions
- Have the children each create a wanted poster for their pirate persona. Be sure to include the reason why they're wanted and how much a reward is. If time allows, have the children go around and introduce their pirate alter egos.

Music (3 minutes)
"A Pirate's Life," from *Disney's Ultimate Swashbuckler Collection* (Walt Disney Records, 2009)

WEEK THREE

Reading Component (5 minutes)
Pirate Girl by Cornelia Funke (Chicken House, 2005)
- This laugh-out-loud story is about a girl who is kidnapped by pirates.

Activity: Create a Paper Boat That Floats (25 minutes)
Supplies
- copies of figure 7.5 (one per child)
  Download full-size pattern from www.alaeditions.org/webextras
- square pieces of paper; you can take computer paper and cut it to 8.5 by 8.5 inches (one per child)

Directions
- Have the children fold the paper as directed in the handout.
- If time allows, fill the bathroom sink with water and see if the boats really float.

Background Music
Caribbean Playground by Putumayo (Putumayo World Music, 2004)

WEEK FOUR

Reading Component (5 minutes)

The Morrow Guide to Knots: For Sailing, Fishing, Camping, Climbing by Mario Bigon and Guido Regazzoni (Collins Reference, 1982)

Activity: Knot Making (25 minutes)

Supplies
- pieces of rope cut to 1-foot lengths; you can find a bolt of clothesline rope at your local hardware store (one per child)

Directions
- If you are not qualified, invite a special guest to come in and teach the children how to tie different knots; a local Boy Scout leader or reservist would be a good candidate. Otherwise, you can use the *Morrow Guide to Knots*. This easy-to-use book has great directions and photographs so you can learn to tie knots.

Background Music

Only One Ocean by Banana Slug String Band (Slug Music, 2011)

BOOKS TO DISPLAY

Adkins, Jan. *What If You Met a Pirate?* Roaring Brook Press, 2006.

Barry, Dave, and Ridley Pearson. *Peter and the Starcatchers*. Hyperion, 2004. (This is one of many in the Peter Pan series.)

Bigon, Mario, and Guido Regazzoni. *The Morrow Guide to Knots: For Sailing, Fishing, Camping, Climbing*. Collins Reference, 1982.

Funke, Cornelia. *Pirate Girl*. Chicken House, 2005.

James, Brian. *The Curse of Snake Island*. Grosset and Dunlap, 2007. (This is one of many in the Pirate School series.)

Kidd, Rob. *The Tale of Billy Turner and Other Stories*. Disney Press, 2009. (This is one of many in the Jack Sparrow series.)

Stevenson, Robert Louis. *Classic Starts: Treasure Island*. Sterling, 2005.

Camp Half-Blood Club (Grades 5–6)

Contributed by Kerry Lemont, Youth Services Assistant, Brookfield Public Library, Brookfield, Illinois.

Program Publicity

Do you feel the need for adventure? Do strange things keep happening to you? Is your math teacher a monster? (No, I mean for real!) Then join us this (season or month) at Camp Half-Blood as we explore the world of Percy Jackson and the Olympians. Discover the Greek god or goddess in your family tree, learn the difference between a centaur and a Minotaur, and undertake new weekly quests for glory.

WEEK ONE

Reading Component (10 minutes)

The Lightning Thief by Rick Riordan (Hyperion, 2005)
- Read pages 78–82 describing Camp Half-Blood.

Activity: Create Cabin Flags (20 minutes)

Supplies
- construction paper
- crayons, colored pencils, or markers
- scissors
- glue

Directions

Ahead of time: Create small strips of paper with god and goddess names on them: Apollo, Hermes, Ares, Dionysus, Aphrodite, Demeter, Hera, Artemis, Athena, Hephaestus.

During the program: Have each child choose a piece of paper to be sorted by cabin. Have supplies ready for each cabin. Instruct the children to create a cabin flag that represents their god or goddess.

Closing Activity: Take-Home Bead (5 minutes)

Each week the kids will decorate a bead and add it to a bracelet to commemorate their time spent in Camp-Half Blood.

Supplies
- pieces of yarn to create either a necklace or bracelet (one per child)
- beads
- glitter markers or permanent markers to decorate beads with

Directions
- Distribute supplies to everyone and let them decorate their beads. (Or you can decorate the beads ahead of time, and just hand them out to the kids on their way out.) The first week's bead is yellow, decorated with a flag.

Background Music

The Best of Authentic Pan Pipes, Flute De Pan by George Schmitt and Santiago (Caravage, 2011)

WEEK TWO

Reading Component (5 minutes)

The Sea of Monsters by Rick Riordan (Hyperion, 2006)
- Read pages 111–115, where they board Princess Andromeda.

Activity: Sea of Monsters Adventure and Trivia Game (25 minutes)

Supplies
- copies of figure 7.6 (one per child)
- copies of figure 7.7, double-sided on cardstock (one per child)
- copies of figure 7.8, double-sided on cardstock (one per child)
- copies of figure 7.9, double-sided on cardstock (one per child)
- copies of figure 7.10, double-sided on cardstock (one per child)
- copies of figure 7.11, double-sided on cardstock (one per child)
- copies of figure 7.12, double-sided on cardstock (one per child)
  Download full-size patterns from www.alaeditions.org/webextras
- dice (you can make copies of figure 1.4 for everyone to create their own dice)

Directions
- You can either print out copies of the board game and let the kids play with others in their cabins, or you can create a life-size board game on the floor.

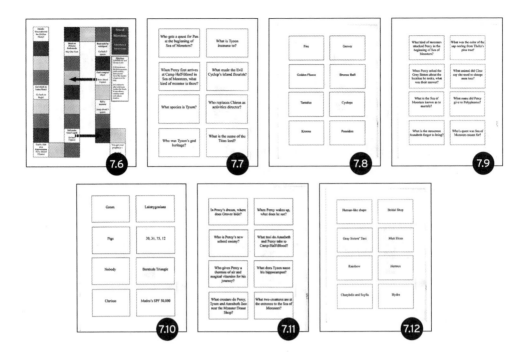

- You can mark out spaces on the floor using painter's tape, or you can use your storytime mats for spaces. If your library space allows you to do a life-size board game, create a PowerPoint with the trivia questions so everybody can read the clues together.
- You can divide the children into their cabins and have them play the game following the rules on the board.

Closing Activity: Take-Home Bead (5 minutes)

This week's bead is red, decorated with dice.

Background Music

The Best of Authentic Pan Pipes, Flute De Pan by George Schmitt and Santiago (Caravage, 2011)

WEEK THREE

Reading Component (10 minutes)

The Titan's Curse by Rick Riordan (Hyperion, 2007)
- Read pages 258–261 about Atlas.

Activity: Holding Up the Sky Relay (15 minutes)

Supplies
- clock or stopwatch
- trash bag filled with pillows (you can bring pillows from home, or ask staff to borrow some)
- painter's or masking tape

Directions
- Divide the group up into their cabins to compete against each other.
- Fill a trash bag with pillows and tie it up. (Have extra bags on hand in case of a tear.)
- Tape two lines on the floor with painter's or masking tape across the room.
- When the stopwatch starts, each team member must carry the bag over his/her head and cross the line on the opposite side of the room and come back to his/her team. They must pass the bag to the next team member without letting it touch the floor. If the bag touches the floor, the team must start over from the beginning while keeping the stopwatch going. The team with the fastest time wins. If teams aren't even with members, you can divide the times by team members to come up with the best average time for the win.

Activity: Greek Shield (15 minutes)

Supplies
- cardstock, posterboard, or cardboard
- crayons, colored pencils, or markers
- construction paper
- glue
- strips of construction paper to hold the shield to the child's arm (two per child)

Directions
- Have children create a circular shield on cardstock, posterboard, or cardboard representing their Greek god family, decorating the shield with a god or protective mythical beast using crayons, colored pencils, or markers.
- Have children glue two strips of construction paper to the back of the shield to hold it to one arm.

Closing Activity: Take-Home Bead (5 minutes)

This week's bead is orange, decorated with a stick figure holding an object over its head.

Background Music

The Best of Authentic Pan Pipes, Flute De Pan by George Schmitt and Santiago (Caravage, 2011)

WEEK FOUR

Reading Component (10 minutes)

The Battle of the Labyrinth by Rick Riordan (Hyperion, 2008)
 – Read pages 348–351, where Annabeth and Percy discuss the prophecy.
The Last Olympian by Rick Riordan (Hyperion, 2009)
 – Read pages 368–370, where Rachel reads the new prophecy to set up the spin-off series.

Activity: Riddles of the Sphinx (10 minutes)

Supplies
 – paper (one sheet per child)
 – pencils

Directions
 – Give the half-bloods a sheet of paper and a pencil to answer the following riddles. You can read them aloud, create a PowerPoint so everyone can read them together, or create a board game.

Riddles

Forward I am heavy, but backward I am not. What am I?
 A ton.

I have a head and feet like a cat, but I am not a cat. What am I?
 A kitten.

If you have it, you want to share it. If you share it, you don't have it. What am I?
 A secret.

I am used to bat with, yet I never get a hit. I am near a ball, yet I am never thrown. What am I?
 An eyelash.

Figure 7.13 Riddles of the Sphinx display

I am broken every time I am spoken. What am I?
> *Silence.*

I have a mouth, but I can't chew. What am I?
> *A river.*

I get wetter and wetter the more I dry. What am I?
> *A towel.*

I can travel around the world while staying in a corner. What am I?
> *A postage stamp.*

Food can help me survive, but water will kill me. What am I?
> *Fire.*

I get whiter the dirtier I get. What am I?
> *A chalkboard.*

I have no beginning, middle, or end. What am I?
> *A doughnut.*

I have to be broken before I can be used. What am I?
> *An egg.*

I go up and never go down. What am I?
>   *Your age.*

I grow when I eat but die when I drink. What am I?
>   *A candle.*

Activity: Create Your Own Oracle (10 minutes)

Supplies
- blank dice (found at educational stores)
- glycerin (a couple of drops per craft: a 4-ounce bottle should suffice for thirty children)
- hot-glue gun
- fine-tip permanent markers
- baby food jars or small mason jars (you can ask the children to each bring one in, or you can collect these ahead of time from staff and story-time patrons)
- construction paper

Directions
Ahead of time: Fill the jars with water and add two drops of glycerin. The jars should be full with no air space left in jar (though small bubbles are okay).

During the program
- Have the children use permanent markers to write prophecy answers on each side of the dice. (Examples: *Yes, No, Maybe, Most likely, Try again, In the future*). Have them place the dice in the water-filled jar and close lid.
- Have the children come to you after they place their dice in the jar. Hot-glue each lid shut.
- Have the children completely cover the jar top and sides with construction paper and decorate. Only the bottom of the jar should remain uncovered.
- To use the Oracle: Ask a yes-or-no question. Shake the jar, turn it upside down, and read your prophecy.

Closing Activity: Take-Home Bead (5 minutes)

This week's bead is green, decorated with a question mark to represent the future.

Background Music

The Best of Authentic Pan Pipes, Flute De Pan by George Schmitt and Santiago (Caravage, 2011)

BOOKS TO DISPLAY

Knight, Mary-Jane. *Percy Jackson and the Olympians: The Ultimate Guide*. Hyperion, 2010.

Riordan, Rick. *The Battle of the Labyrinth*. Hyperion, 2008.

Riordan, Rick. *Demigods and Monsters: Your Favorite Authors on Rick Riordan's Percy Jackson and the Olympians Series*. Smart Pop, 2009.

Riordan, Rick. *The Last Olympian*. Hyperion, 2009.

Riordan, Rick. *The Lightning Thief*. Hyperion, 2005. (This is one of many in the Percy Jackson series.)

Riordan, Rick. *The Lightning Thief: The Graphic Novel*. Hyperion, 2010.

Riordan, Rick. *The Lost Hero*. Hyperion, 2010. (This is one of many in the Heroes of Olympus series.)

Riordan, Rick. *The Sea of Monsters*. Hyperion, 2006.

Riordan, Rick. *The Titan's Curse*. Hyperion, 2007.

Chapter 8

Adventures

WHO DOESN'T LOVE AN ADVENTURE? CHILDREN ARE ALWAYS CREATING THEIR own adventures while playing in the backyard or on the playground. Bring the adventure of reading to them every week. Transport the younger ones on animal adventures, take spy excursions around the world with second and third graders, and teach survival skills to soon-to-be-middle schoolers with the power of reading.

Adventure Club (Grades K–2)

Program Publicity

Crocs and tigers and snakes—oh my! Join the Adventure Club at the XYZ Library and listen to stories including *The Secret Shortcut, The Dangerous Snake and Reptile Club, Little White Rabbit,* and *Shark vs. Train.* Go through a secret shortcut to school, imagine being a little white rabbit, and see who wins in a shark-versus-train match. Create crafts such as a jungle dice game, a snake action figure, a little white rabbit illustration, and a shark and train stick puppet.

WEEK ONE

Reading Component (5 minutes)

The Secret Shortcut by Mark Teague (Scholastic, 1999)
  – Two friends find a "shortcut" to school and are inevitably late.

Activity: Jungle Match (25 minutes)

Supplies
- copies of figure 8.1 (one per child)
- copies of figure 8.2 (one per child)
  Download full-size patterns from www.alaeditions.org/webextras
- crayons, colored pencils, or markers
- scissors
- tape

8.1   8.2

Directions
- Have the children color the animals using crayons, colored pencils, or markers.
- Have them cut out the two cross-shaped activity sheets.
- Have them fold the sheets on each black line, using tape to hold the edges of the squares together to create the dice.
- To play: The children roll the dice until they make a match of each of the jungle animals: crocodile, tiger, snake, monkey, elephant, and rhinoceros. Have the kids compete to see who can match all the animals first.

Music (3 minutes)

"Mister" by Laurie Berkner, from *Under a Shady Tree* (Two Tomatoes, 2002)
- Dance and act like a chimpanzee, parakeet, elephant, and alien to complement the silly adventure story.

WEEK TWO

Reading Component (5 minutes)

The Dangerous Snake and Reptile Club by Daniel San Souci (Tricycle Press, 2004)
- This picture book describes a club that every child joins at some point in their childhood.

Activity: Snake Action Figure (25 minutes)

Supplies
- copies of figure 8.3 on cardstock
  (one sheet makes six different snakes;
  one snake per child)
  *Download full-size pattern from
  www.alaeditions.org/webextras*
- construction paper in various colors cut into
  1-by-12-inch strips (two per child)
- googly eyes (optional; two per child)
- glue
- scissors
- tape

Directions
- Have the children cut out the snake head.
- Have them weave together the two strips
  of construction paper in an accordion pattern.
- Have them tape the snake head to one end of
  the construction paper weave.
- Have them glue googly eyes on the snake head for an extra pop.
- If you need to fill extra time, hand out extra construction paper strips to
  see who can weave the longest snake.

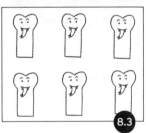

Music (3 minutes)

"Old MacDonald's Band" by Hap Palmer, from *Rhythms on Parade* (Hap-Pal
  Music, 1995)
- A rattlesnake enters Old MacDonald's Band in this little ditty. Break out
  your musical instruments for this one.

WEEK THREE

Reading Component (5 minutes)

Little White Rabbit by Kevin Henkes (Greenwillow Books, 2011)
- The little white rabbit imagines what it's like to be a rock, to fly, and to
  be a giant.

Activity: Create Your Own White Rabbit (25 minutes)

Supplies
- construction paper
- crayons, colored pencils, or markers

Directions
- Tell the children to imagine something new for Little White Rabbit. Imagine he was like a flower, or could swim underwater. Have them draw what it would be like for White Rabbit. Allow enough time to let each child have a turn to show-and-tell their drawing.

Music (3 minutes)

"Fast and Slow" by Laurie Berkner, from *Rocketship Run* (Razor and Tie, 2008)
- Pass out shakers so the kids can pretend to be a fast rabbit and a slow turtle.

WEEK FOUR

Reading Component (5 minutes)

Shark vs. Train by Chris Barton (Little, Brown, 2010)
- There are different contests in which Shark and Train compete in this funny story.

Activity: Shark vs. Train Stick Puppets (25 minutes)

Supplies
- copies of figure 8.4 (one per child; copy on blue or gray paper if you want to add color) *Download full-size pattern from www.alaeditions.org/webextras*

- scissors
- tape
- craft sticks (two per child)
- crayons, colored pencils, or markers

Directions
- Have the children color the shark and the train and then cut them out.
- Have them tape one craft stick to the shark and one to the train. (Glue takes too long to dry, so use tape!)

Music (3 minutes)

"Ready, Set, Move!" by Greg and Steve, from *Ready . . . Set . . . Move!* (Greg and Steve Productions, 2004)
   – Let the kids dance and pretend with their new stick puppets.

BOOKS TO DISPLAY

Axtell, David. *We're Going on a Lion Hunt*. Henry Holt, 2007.

Barton, Chris. *Shark vs. Train*. Little, Brown Books for Young Readers, 2010.

Henkes, Kevin. *Little White Rabbit*. Greenwillow Books, 2011.

Matieu, Matt. *We're Going on a Lion Hunt*. Marshall Cavendish, 2008.

Rosen, Michael. *We're Going on a Bear Hunt*. Margaret K. McElderry, 2009.

San Souci, Daniel. *The Dangerous Snake and Reptile Club*. Tricycle Press, 2004.

Sendak, Maurice. *Where the Wild Things Are*. HarperCollins, 1988.

Teague, Mark. *The Secret Shortcut*. Scholastic, 1999.

Van Allsburg, Chris. *Jumanji*. Houghton Mifflin Books for Children, 1981.

Van Allsburg, Chris. *Zathura*. Houghton Mifflin Books for Children, 2002.

Wiesner, David. *Sector 7*. Clarion, 1999.

Secret Agent Jack Stalwart Club

(Grades 3–4)

Contributed by Elizabeth Esposito, Youth and Teen Librarian, South Huntington Public Library in Huntington Station, New York.

Program Publicity

Pssst . . . secret agents: Want to hang out with other secret agents who share your love for global adventure, cool gadgets, and crime solving? Then the Jack Stalwart Club is for you! Join us each week at the XYZ Library to track down interesting new books, play games, create crafts, and try out spy stuff.

WEEK ONE

Reading Component (5 minutes)

The Secret of the Sacred Temple by Elizabeth Singer Hunt (Weinstein Books, 2008)

– Read chapter 5, when Jack first learns about Angkor Wat.

Activity: Create Your Own Angkor Wat (25 minutes)

Supplies
- 2 cups of flour (one 5-pound bag makes nine batches)
- 1 cup salt
- ½–¾ cup water
- measuring cup
- mixing bowl
- food coloring (optional)

Directions
- You can create homemade salt dough ahead of time, or you can mix it up in front of the children so they know how to make it. This recipe can air-dry, so you don't need an oven to bake the temples. Children can take these home and let them dry overnight. If you have a large group of thirty children, you can let each table make their own recipe to make a big Cambodian temple. Allow it to air-dry, then display their creations around the library.
- Mix the flour and salt together in the mixing bowl. Slowly add ½ cup of water.

– Knead the dough. If it's too dry slowly add more water.
– If you want to color the dough, use food coloring.

Background Music

Echoes from the Palace: Court Music of Cambodia by Sam-Ang Ensemble (Music of the World, 1999)

WEEK TWO

Reading Component (5 minutes)

The Caper of the Crown Jewels by Elizabeth Singer Hunt (Weinstein Books, 2008)
– Read chapter 4, where the crown jewels are stolen.

Activity: JEWEL Bingo (25 minutes)

Supplies

– copy of figure 8.5
– copies of figure 8.6
  (one per child)
  *Download full-size patterns
  from www.alaeditions.org/
  webextras*
– square markers measuring 1
  inch by 1 inch (25 per child)

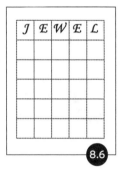

Directions

Ahead of time: Print out figure 8.5 and cut out numbers 1–50. Place them in a cup or a hat. Cut out square markers measuring 1 inch by 1 inch for the children to use when their number is called. You can place a pile of these markers in the center of the table for use. If you have money in the budget to splurge, you can give out stickers or jewels to use as markers.

During the program: Tell the children to fill out their own bingo cards using numbers 1–50. (You must *not* repeat any numbers.)

You can play bingo one of two ways:

Line Bingo: Make a horizontal, vertical or diagonal line to create one JEWEL bingo.

Blackout Bingo: Every square, totaling 25, must be completed to create a JEWEL bingo.

When a child gets a bingo, instruct them to yell out, "Jewel!" You can have silly prizes, such as crowns or jewels, to give away for the winners if you have money to splurge with— or use up those leftover mismatched incentives from past programs that you don't know what to do with.

Background Music
The Beatles 1 by the Beatles (Apple, 2000)

WEEK THREE

Reading Component (5 minutes)
The Puzzle of the Missing Panda by Elizabeth Singer Hunt (Weinstein Books, 2008)
  – Read chapter 6, where Jack uses his secret language decoder to listen to Wong and Wong.

Activity: Secret Decoder Necklace (25 minutes)

Supplies

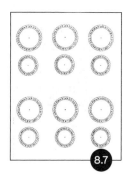

  – copies of figure 8.7 (one sheet will make six crafts; one craft per child)
  – copies of figure 8.8
    (one per child)
    Download full-size patterns from www.alaeditions.org/webextras
  – string cut to 28-inch lengths (one per child)
  – paper clips (one per child)
  – brads (one per child)
  – tape

Directions
  – Have the children cut out the secret decoder circles.
  – Have them poke tiny holes in the center of each circle.
  – Have them place a brad through the center of both circles to secure them together.
  – Have them tape the paper clip to the back of the pendant to create a "jump ring" to string the necklace to the pendant.

Background Music
Asian Dreamland by Putumayo Presents (Putumayo World Music, 2006)

WEEK FOUR

Reading Component (5 minutes)

The Search for Sunken Treasure by Elizabeth Singer Hunt (Weinstein Books, 2007)
  - Read chapter 1, which introduces the amazing sea life that lives in the Great Barrier Reef.

Activity: Make Your Own Coral Reef Diorama (25 minutes)

Supplies
  - shoe box or cereal box (one per table)
  - blue paint or tissue paper to create an underwater feel
  - glue
  - scissors
  - various craft supplies such as paper towel rolls, pasta, and construction paper to create sea anemones, coral sponges, sea fans, and fish

Directions
  - Prop up the shoe box on its side to create a diorama. If you're using a cereal box, have the children cut a rectangle from the front of the cereal box and prop the box on its side.
  - Have the children paint the box blue to create the underwater feel. If you don't want to wait for paint to dry, have them glue blue tissue paper to the box.
  - Have the children use various craft supplies to create a coral reef. Allow them to use their imaginations and be creative!

Background Music

Bush Songs from the Australian Outback by Aussie Bush Band (Collectables Records, 2007)

BOOKS TO DISPLAY

Black, Holly, and Tony DiTerlizzi. *The Field Guide.* Simon and Schuster, 2003. (This is one of many in the Spiderwick series.)

Burnford, Sheila. *Incredible Journey.* Yearling, 1997.

Clements, Andrew. *A Week in the Woods.* Atheneum, 2004.

Hunt, Elizabeth Singer. *The Caper of the Crown Jewels.* Weinstein Books, 2008.

Hunt, Elizabeth Singer. *The Escape of the Deadly Dinosaur.* Weinstein Books, 2007.

Hunt, Elizabeth Singer. *The Puzzle of the Missing Panda.* Weinstein Books, 2008.

Hunt, Elizabeth Singer. *The Secret of the Sacred Temple.* Weinstein Books, 2008.

Korman, Gordon. *Shipwreck.* Scholastic, 2001. (This is one of many in the Shipwreck series.)

Law, Ingrid. *Savvy.* Puffin, 2010.

Lindgren, Astrid. *Pippi Longstocking.* Puffin, 2005.

McMann, Lisa. *The Unwanteds.* Aladdin, 2012.

Miller, Wiley. *Extraordinary Adventures of Ordinary Basil.* Blue Sky Press, 2006.

Tweens versus Wild Club (Grades 5–6)

Program Publicity

Imagine you're stranded in the woods with the bare necessities. How would you survive? Read about tales of survival and learn secrets to survival in the Tweens versus Wild Club at the XYZ Library. Create your own survival tin, compass, fishing pole, and thermometer with this club. Learn literary characters' survival tales, including Brian Robeson, Sam Gribley, Miyax, and Stanley Yelnats. Please register early for this program—we will need a head count to purchase the correct number of survival supplies.

WEEK ONE

Reading Component (5 minutes)
Hatchet by Gary Paulsen (Scholastic, 1999)
   – Read chapter 5, when Brian wakes up from the plane crash and looks for water.

Activity: Survival Tin (25 minutes)
Supplies
   – mint tin or small jewelry box to hold valuable items (one per child)
   – Band-Aids (a few per child)
   – copies of figure 8.9 (one per child)
     Download full-size pattern from www.alaeditions.org/webextras
   – aluminum foil in 1-foot squares to create cups (one per child)
   – construction paper
   – glue
   – crayons, colored pencils, or markers

Directions
- Have the children glue pieces of construction paper on the tin and decorate it.
- Have them create an aluminum cup and fold it to fit inside the survival tin.
- Have them add Band-Aids and other valuables to the tin.

Background Music
Forest Sounds: With Soft Rains and Gentle Winds by Rest and Relax Artist Series (Robbins Island Music, 2010)

WEEK TWO

Reading Component (5 minutes)
My Side of the Mountain by Jean Craighead George (Puffin, 2004)
- Start at page 9, "In which I get started on this venture," when Sam packs up and leaves for the Catskill Mountains.

Activity: Compass (25 minutes)
Supplies
- magnets (one per table)
- sewing needles (one per table)
- cups of water (one per table)
- cork or small piece of Styrofoam (you can break apart a Styrofoam plate)

Figure 8.10 Compass floating in cup

Directions
- Have the children turn the needle into a magnet by rubbing the needle against the magnet fifty times in one direction (not back and forth).
- Have them place the needle in the middle of the water glass, getting it to float on the surface. Inform them to be patient and try to avoid any kind of wind.
- If the needle doesn't float on the surface, have the children float a cork or piece of Styrofoam, then place the needle on top of it.
- The needle will slowly rotate toward the north.

Background Music
Echoes of Nature: Wild Animals (Cobra Entertainment, 1993)

WEEK THREE

Reading Component (5 minutes)
Julie of the Wolves by Jean Craighead George (HarperCollins, 1999)
- Read pages 5–10, where Miyax describes communicating with the wolf, Amaroq.

Activity: Bottle Fishing Pole (25 minutes)

Supplies
- plastic water or soda bottles (one per child)
- paper clips to use as fishing hooks (one per child)
- aluminum foil—gum wrappers or tiny pieces of foil—for lures (one per child)
- fishing line cut to 6-foot lengths (one per child)
- packing tape
- permanent markers (optional)
- stickers (optional)

Figure 8.11 Bottle fishing pole

Directions
- Have the children tape one end of the fishing line to the center of the plastic bottle.
- Have them wrap the line around the bottle.
- Have them tie the paper clip to the other end.
- Have them add the lure (from a piece of aluminum foil) to the paper clip.
- Have the children hold the bottle upside down and practice throwing their lines. Set up an X on the floor for children to practice with. To lengthen this activity, have the children decorate their bottles with permanent markers or stickers.

Background Music
Sounds of the Earth: Wolves by Sounds of the Earth (Oreade Music, 1999)

WEEK FOUR

Reading Component (5 minutes)

Holes by Louis Sachar (Farrar, Straus and Giroux, 1998)
- Read chapter 5, where Stanley meets Barf Bag, Squid, X-Ray, Magnet, Armpit, Zigzag, and Zero. Ask the kids how they would survive with these characters.

Activity: Thermometer (25 minutes)

Supplies
- plastic water or soda bottles (one per child)
- water (½ cup per child)
- rubbing alcohol, blue or green in color if you can find it (½ cup per child)
- food coloring (optional, if you can't find colored alcohol)
- measuring cup
- transparent plastic drinking straws (one per child)
- small piece of clay (one per child)
- permanent marker

Figure 8.12 Bottle thermometer

Directions
- If you couldn't find colored rubbing alcohol, pour a few drops of food coloring into the rubbing alcohol bottles. (This will make it easier to read the temperature.)
- Measure out ½ cups of rubbing alcohol for each child to pour into their bottles.
- Measure out ½ cups of water for each child to pour into their bottles.
- Have the children place a straw in each bottle, but don't let it touch the bottom. Keep the straw about a half-inch from the bottom.
- Have them seal the straw in the neck of the bottle with modeling clay, keeping the straw straight and stable.
- Have them warm the bottom of the bottle with their hands to watch the liquid rise up the straw. (The straw is the thermometer.)
- Allow the thermometer to sit at room temperature for five minutes.
- Have the children mark the temperature on the outside of the bottle with a line. Instruct the children to mark the outside of the bottle at home with different degrees to they can read the thermometer each day.

Background Music

Healing Sounds of Nature: Thunderstorm, Rain, and Ocean Waves by Music for
Deep Sleep (Inner Splendor Media, 2008)

BOOKS TO DISPLAY

Avi. *The True Confessions of Charlotte Doyle*. HarperCollins, 2004.

Bosch, Pseudonymous. *The Name of This Book Is Secret*. Little, Brown Books for
Young Readers, 2008. (This is one of many in the Secret series.)

Easton, Kelly. *Outlandish Adventures of Liberty Aimes*. Yearling, 2011.

Fardell, John. *Professors of the Far North*. Puffin, 2006.

George, Jean Craighead. *Julie of the Wolves*. HarperCollins, 1999.

George, Jean Craighead. *My Side of the Mountain*. Puffin, 2004.

Paulsen, Gary. *Hatchet*. Scholastic, 1999.

Ryan, Pam Munoz. *Paint the Wind*. Scholastic, 2009.

Sachar, Louis. *Holes*. Farrar, Straus and Giroux, 1998.

Salisbury, Graham. *Night of the Howling Dog*. Laurel Leaf, 2009.

Smith, Roland. *Peak*. Harcourt, 2008.

Taylor, Theodore. *The Cay*. Laurel Leaf, 2003.

Chapter 9

School

THE FALL IS THE PERFECT TIME TO DO A SCHOOL-THEMED PROGRAM BEFORE the excitement wears off. Usually children are ready to get back into the routine after a long summer. Share school stories with them and help them get ready for the year by making appropriate crafts. You can even use these ideas to do a "summer school," where you do the program in four consecutive days before the beginning of the school-year kickoff.

Back to School Club (Grades K–2)

Program Publicity

Get ready for your new school year at the XYZ Library. Create back-to-school crafts to get you organized for the fall. Make a pencil cup, decorate lunch bags, construct pencil wrappers, and embellish a bookmark. Listen to school stories including *If You Take a Mouse to School*, *First Day Jitters*, *Miss Nelson Is Missing*, and *A Fine, Fine School*. Sing songs about the new year such as "School Quiz," "The First 12 Days of School," and "There's a Dog in School."

WEEK ONE

Reading Component (5 minutes)

A Fine, Fine School by Sharon Creech (HarperCollins, 2001)
– A principal is so proud of his school, he thinks everyone should attend all year-round with no weekends or vacations.

Activity: Pencil Holder Decorating (25 minutes)

Supplies
- paper cups (two per child)
- tissue paper or old magazines (you can use weeded copies or ask each child to bring one)
- white glue
- water
- measuring cup (optional)

Directions
- Each child should take one paper cup and add a mixture of half white glue and half water to make a papier-mâché adhesive. You can use measuring cups, or you can estimate. As long as you have equal parts the adhesive solution will work just fine.
- Tear small squares of tissue paper or magazine pages.
- Have the children dip the tissue paper or magazine squares into the adhesive mixture.
- Have them place the tissue paper and magazine squares on the outside of the other paper cup to create a collage.
- Let the adhesive dry. The children can use the cup as a pencil holder.

Music (3 minutes)

"School Quiz" by Kimbo, from *People in Our Neighborhood* (Kimbo, 2000)
- Guess which community helpers the singer sings about, including a teacher, librarian, principal, and crossing guard.

WEEK TWO

Reading Component (5 minutes)

If You Take a Mouse to School by Laura Numeroff (HarperCollins, 2002)
- This circular story describes a mouse going to school on his first day.

Activity: Lunch Bag Decorating (25 minutes)

Supplies
- lunch bags (five per child)
- crayons, colored pencils, or markers
- stickers (optional)

Directions
- Give the children time to decorate a week's worth of lunch bags to bring to school. They can use Numeroff's book for inspiration on decorating ideas.

Music (5 minutes)

"The First 12 Days of School" by Dr. Jean, from *Keep on Singing and Dancing with Dr. Jean* (Melody House, 2007)
- Sing about ABC books, pencils, crayons, and glue sticks in this school-themed version of "The Twelve Days of Christmas."

WEEK THREE

Reading Component (5 minutes)

First Day Jitters by Julie Danneberg (Charlesbridge, 2000)
- This surprise ending describes the stress and anxiety of the first day. (The point of view is from a teacher!)

Activity: Pencil Wrappers (25 minutes)

Supplies
- chenille stems
- pony beads (forty per child)
- pencils, either library promotional pencils or ones that children bring in from home (one per child)

Directions
- Have the children lace beads onto the chenille stem in any pattern they want. Have them twist the ends of the pipe cleaner so the beads won't come off.
- Have them twist the pipe cleaner around the pencil.

Music (4 minutes)

"The First Day of School" by Kimbo, from *We've Got Harmony* (Kimbo, 2007)
- Pretend you're getting ready for the first day of school and act out getting dressed and waiting for the bus.

WEEK FOUR

Reading Component (5 minutes)

Miss Nelson Is Missing by Harry Allard (Houghton Mifflin, 1977)
- A teacher, tired of her students' bad behavior, comes to school as a mean substitute to change her class's attitude.

Activity: Bookmark or Shelf Marker (25 minutes)

Supplies
- construction paper cut into 2-by-11-inch strips (one per child)
- crayons, colored pencils, or markers

Directions
- Have the children decorate the strips of construction paper using crayons, colored pencils, or markers.
- These can be used either as bookmarks or shelf markers to use in the library.

Music (5 minutes)

"There's a Dog in School" by Carole Peterson, from *H.U.M.: Highly Usable Music All Year Long* (Carole Peterson, 2004)
- Woof, meow, quack, hop, and sing the alphabet with various animals.

BOOKS TO DISPLAY

Allard, Harry. *Miss Nelson Is Missing*. Houghton Mifflin, 1977.

Creech, Sharon. *A Fine, Fine School*. HarperCollins, 2001.

Danneberg, Julie. *First Day Jitters*. Charlesbridge, 2000.

London, Jonathan. *Froggy Goes to School*. Viking Juvenile, 1996.

Mayer, Mercer. *First Day of School*. Harper Festival, 2009.

Numeroff, Laura. *If You Take a Mouse to School*. HarperCollins, 2002.

Parish, Herman. *Amelia Bedelia's First Day of School*. Greenwillow, 2011.

Rey, Margaret and H. A. *Curious George's First Day of School*. HMH Books, 2005.

Thompson, Lauren. *Mouse's First Day of School*. Simon and Schuster, 2003.

Wing, Natasha. *The Night before First Grade*. Grosset and Dunlap, 2005.

Yolen, Jane. *How Do Dinosaurs Go to School?* Blue Sky Press, 2007.

Crafty Kids Club (Grades 3–4)

Program Publicity

Get ready for the new school year with the Crafty Kids Club at the XYZ Library. Create back-to-school crafts to use in your classroom, including a journal, a backpack dangler, a decorated folder, and a craft stick photo frame. Enjoy stories from the Big Nate and My Weird School. Join the fun by registering at the XYZ Library before (date).

WEEK ONE

Reading Component (5 minutes)

The Principal's New Clothes by Stephanie Calmenson (Scholastic, 1991)
   – A school take on the "Emperor's New Clothes."

Activity: Backpack Dangler (25 minutes)

Supplies
   – pony beads (forty per child—if you can get ahold of alphabet beads or decorative beads, the kids will love them!)
   – safety pins (five per child)
   – paper plates or small cups
   – ribbon, string, or yarn
   – hot glue or crazy glue (optional)

Figure 9.1 Backpack dangler

Directions
   – Distribute the pony beads on paper plates, or fill up small cups for each child.
   – Have the children open up one safety pin to be the Dangler.
   – Have them bead the other four safety pins.
   – Have them thread the ends of the four decorated safety pins onto the Dangler, then close the pin.
   – If you wish, you can seal the pins closed with either hot glue or crazy glue.
   – Have the children tie a ribbon, string, or yarn to the top of the Dangler and attach it to a backpack.

Background Music

High School Musical (Walt Disney Records, 2006)

WEEK TWO

Reading Component (5 minutes)

Big Nate in a Class by Himself by Lincoln Peirce (United Feature Syndicate, 2010)
- Read pages 1–7, where Nate has nightmares about getting called on from his teacher for an answer.

Activity: Craft Stick Picture Frame (25 minutes)

Supplies
- craft sticks (eight per child)
- glue
- stickers
- markers

Directions
- Have the children glue two craft sticks together side by side, making four sets.
- Have them glue the sets together to create a frame.
- Have them decorate the frame with markers and stickers.

Background Music

High School Musical 2 (Walt Disney Records, 2007)

WEEK THREE

Reading Component (5 minutes)

Miss Daisy Is Crazy! by Dan Gutman (Harper Trophy, 2004)
- Read chapter 1, where A. J. describes Miss Daisy not liking school and wanting to stay home eating bonbons all day long.

Activity: Folder Decorating (25 minutes)

Supplies
- folders (one per child)
- markers
- stickers

Directions
Allow plenty of time for the kids to use markers and stickers to decorate a brand-new folder for school.

Background Music

High School Musical 3: Senior Year (Walt Disney Records, 2008)

WEEK FOUR

Reading Component (5 minutes)

The School for the Insanely Gifted by Dan Elish (HarperCollins, 2011)
- Read chapter 1, where Daphna describes her unique traits and her Blatt School for the Insanely Gifted.

Activity: Composition Book Decorating (25 minutes)

Supplies
- composition journals (one per child; you can also ask each child to bring one)
- markers
- stickers
- glitter pens

Directions
- Allow the children plenty of time to use markers, stickers, and glitter pens to decorate a new notebook for school.

Background Music

Camp Rock (Walt Disney Records, 2008)

BOOKS TO DISPLAY

Adler, Susan S. *Samantha Learns a Lesson*. American Girl Publishing, 1986.

Avi. *The Secret School*. Sandpiper, 2003.

Calmenson, Stephanie. *The Principal's New Clothes*. Scholastic, 1991.

Dahl, Connie. *Addy Learns a Lesson*. American Girl Publishing, 1993.

Elish, Dan. *The School for the Insanely Gifted*. HarperCollins, 2011.

Gutman, Dan. *Miss Daisy Is Crazy!* Harper Trophy, 2004. (This is one of many in the My Weird School series.)

McMullan, Kate. *School! Adventures at the Harvey N. Trouble Elementary School*. Feiwel and Friends, 2010.

McNaughton, Colin. *Captain Abdul's Pirate School*. Candlewick, 2004.

Peirce, Lincoln. *Big Nate in a Class by Himself*. United Feature Syndicate, 2010. (This is one of many in the Big Nate series.)

Shaw, Janet Beeler. *Kirsten Learns a Lesson*. American Girl Publishing, 1986.

Tripp, Valerie. *Felicity Learns a Lesson*. American Girl Publishing, 1991.

Tripp, Valerie. *Josefina Learns a Lesson*. American Girl Publishing, 1997.

Tripp, Valerie. *Kit Learns a Lesson*. American Girl Publishing, 2000.

Tween Club (Grades 5–6)

Program Publicity

Create back-to-school crafts to use in the classroom this fall at the XYZ Library. Decorate a binder and a locker mirror, create a note holder, and learn how to cover your textbooks. Listen to school stories about Regnie, Sadeed, the D Squad, and Daphna and their unique situations—including pen pals from across the globe, a machine that does your homework for you, and gifted and talented programs. Sign up by (date).

WEEK ONE

Reading Component (5 minutes)

The Fabled Fifth Graders of Aesop Elementary School by Candace Fleming (Schwartz and Wade, 2010)
  – Read pages 16–20, "Class Curriculum," where Mr. Jupiter tells the class they'll learn about the life cycle of Bigfoot and six ways to look for extra-terrestrial life this year.

Activity: Book Covers (25 minutes)

Supplies
- brown paper grocery bags (one per child)
- scissors
- tape
- crayons, colored pencils, or markers

Directions
- Teach the children how to cover a book. You can always teach one child from each table and have them help their tablemates, or have teen volunteers come in to help you with this program.
- Allow the children time to decorate their new covers.
- Optional: You can use a projector to show instructions to the children. You can also search online on YouTube for "paper bag book cover" or go to http://familycrafts.about.com/od/homemadebooks/ss/PBBookCover.htm for instructions.

Background Music
50 Classical Highlights: Essential Classics (St. Clair Entertainment, 2002)

WEEK TWO

Reading Component (5 minutes)
The Mysterious Benedict Society by Trenton Lee Stewart (Little, Brown, 2007)
- Read pages 9–14, beginning with "It was a curious test," when Reynie explains the test after seeing an ad for a gifted child looking for special opportunities.

Activity: Locker Mirror (25 minutes)

Supplies
- mirrors (one per child)
- foam stickers
- markers

Directions
- Have the children use stickers and markers to decorate mirrors for their school lockers.

Background Music
The Most Relaxing Piano Album in the World (EMI Classics, 2001)

WEEK THREE

Reading Component (5 minutes)

The Homework Machine by Dan Gutman (Simon and Schuster Books for Young
Readers, 2006)
  – Read chapter 2, where the kids describe the homework machine working
    for the first time. If you have a group of kids who are comfortable read-
    ing aloud, pass the book around to hear the different voices featured in
    the story.

Activity: Binder Decorating (25 minutes)

Supplies
  – binders (one per child)
  – markers
  – glitter pens

Directions
  – Allow the children plenty of time to decorate their new binders with
    markers and glitter pens.

Background Music

Symphony Favorites (Vox, 1997)

WEEK FOUR

Reading Component (5 minutes)

Extra Credit by Andrew Clements (Atheneum Books for Young Readers, 2009)
  – Read chapter 1, where Sadeed is given an important job of being a pen-
    pal to an American girl.

Activity: Post-It Note Holder (25 minutes)

Supplies
  – copies of figure 9.2 on cardstock (one per child)
    Download full-size pattern from www.alaeditions
    .org/webextras
  – scissors
  – crayons, colored pencils, or markers

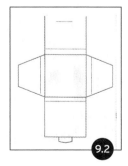

9.2

Directions
- – Have the children cut out the pattern and fold it on the dotted lines.
- – Have them create one slit in the small horizontal line in the top square to keep closed.
- – Have them decorate their note holder using crayons, colored pencils, or markers.

Background Music
25 Children's Favorites (Vox, 2000)

BOOKS TO DISPLAY

Clements, Andrew. *Extra Credit.* Atheneum Books for Young Readers, 2009.

Clements, Andrew. *We the Children.* Atheneum Books for Young Readers, 2011.

Daneshvari, Gitty. *School of Fear.* Little, Brown Books for Young Readers, 2011. (This is one of many in the School of Fear series.)

Epstein, Robin. *The Worst-Case Scenario Survival Handbook: Middle School.* Chronicle, 2009.

Fleming, Candace. *The Fabled Fifth Graders of Aesop Elementary School.* Schwartz and Wade, 2010.

Gutman, Dan. *The Homework Machine.* Simon and Schuster Books for Young Readers, 2006.

Patterson, James. *Middle School: The Worst Years of My Life.* Little, Brown Books for Young Readers, 2011.

Stein, R. L. *It's the First Day of School . . . Forever!* Feiwel and Friends, 2011.

Stewart, Trenton Lee. *The Mysterious Benedict Society.* Little, Brown, 2007. (This is one of many in the Mysterious Benedict series.)

Chapter 10

Chillers

THERE ARE SO MANY GOOD SCARY STORIES FOR CHILDREN NOWADAYS. READ-ing aloud a story that builds suspense is so much fun. Teaching children the element of surprise will be a blast using these spooky program ideas. These programs appeal to both genders while easing anxiety about certain fears, including hearing noises from under the bed and being in the dark.

Monster Mash Club (Grades K–2)

Program Publicity
Listen to spooky stories throughout the month of October at the XYZ Library. Sing songs about monsters and "invent" crafts that would make Frankenstein proud. Learn storytelling and create a Wild Thing costume. Please register for this event by calling the library or registering at our website.

WEEK ONE

Reading Component (5 minutes)
There Was an Old Monster! by Adrian, Ed, and Rebecca Emberley (Orchard Books, 2009)
- A new twist on the Old Lady Who Swallowed a Fly.

Activity: There Was an Old Monster Puppet (25 minutes)

Supplies
- copies of figure 10.1 (one per child)
- copies of figure 10.2 (one per child)
  Download full-size patterns from www.alaeditions.org/ webextras
- crayons, colored pencil, or markers
- scissors
- brads (one per child)

Directions
- Have the children color the monster and the animals he eats using crayons, colored pencils, or markers.
- Have them cut out the circles on each page.
- Have them poke a hole in the center of the circles, making sure the monster is on top.
- Have them place the brad in the center and fasten.

Music (2 minutes)

"Monster Boogie" by Laurie Berkner, from *The Best of the Laurie Berkner Band* (Two Tomatoes, 2010)
- Stomp and wiggle while showing your green teeth and purple eyes in this little ditty.

WEEK TWO

Reading Component (5 minutes)

The Great Monster Hunt by Norbert Landa (Good Books, 2010)
- Duck hears a noise under the bed, and all his friends help him catch the "monster" (a snoring mouse).

Activity: Monster-Catcher Net (25 minutes)

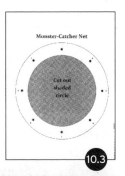

Supplies
- copies of figure 10.3 on cardstock or construction
  paper (one per child)
  *Download full-size pattern from
  www.alaeditions.org/webextras*
- yarn cut to 24-inch lengths (four
  per child)
- scissors
- hole punch
- crayons, colored pencils, or markers
- tape
- craft stick (one per child)

Directions

Ahead of time: Ask a volunteer to prep these
monster nets: Cut along outside line of circle
from figure 10.3. Poke a hole in the center of

Figure 10.4 Monster-Catcher Net

the shaded circle and cut along inside the line, leaving a frame for the monster-
catcher net. Using a hole punch, punch eight holes at the marked spots. Cut four
pieces of yarn for each child in 24-inch lengths.

During the program: Have the children decorate the monster net using crayons,
colored pencils, or markers.
- Have them thread a piece of yarn from hole #1 to hole #1, using tape
  to secure and leaving yarn hanging through the bottom. Repeat with the
  other pieces of yarn, securing #2 to #2, #3 to #3, and #4 to #4.
- Have the children tape a craft stick to one edge to create a monster-
  catcher net.

Music (2 minutes)

"Going on a Hunt (Blues)" by Laurie Berkner, from *Rocketship Run* (Razor and
Tie, 2008)
- Use your new monster-catcher while acting out this song. You can hide a
  matchbox with a mouse sleeping in it to coordinate with the story.

WEEK THREE

Reading Component (5 minutes)
Annie Was Warned by Jarrett J. Krosoczka (Alfred A. Knopf, 2003)
- Suspense builds in this surprise-ending story.

Activity: Flashlight Stories (25 minutes)

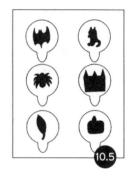

Supplies
- copies of figure 10.5 on cardstock (one per child)
  Download full-size pattern from www.alaeditions .org/webextras
- scissors
- flashlight (you can use one for demonstration purposes)

Directions
- Have the children cut out the six circular shapes, leaving the thumb holders.
- Have them poke a hole through each black figure and cut out around the black lines, leaving only the white cardstock.
- Hold up one figure against the front of a flashlight in a dark room.
- Allow time for the children to practice telling the story using the flashlight figures.

Music (3 minutes)
"Monster Boogies" by Kiddle Karoo, from *Silly Monster House Party* (Silly Monsters, 2010)
- This is a monster version of the hokey pokey.

WEEK FOUR

Reading Component (5 minutes)
Where the Wild Things Are by Maurice Sendak (HarperCollins, 1988)
- Max goes on an imaginative journey after being sent to his room.

Activity: Wild Thing Mask and Feet (25 minutes)
Supplies
- copies of figure 10.6 on white cardstock (one per child)
- copies of figure 10.7 on various colors of cardstock (one per child)
- copies of figure 10.8 on various colors of cardstock (one per child)

- scissors
- dinner-size paper plates in various colors (one per child)
- hole punch
- glue
- yarn cut to 3-inch lengths (sixty per child: thirty for the mask and fifteen for each foot)
- yarn cut to 24-inch lengths to tie around the head (one per child)

  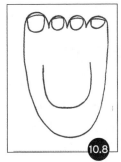

Directions for Wild Thing Mask

Ahead of time: Cut out eye holes for the mask. You can do this ahead of time, or have teen volunteers do it for you. You can create a template using one plate and trace the eye holes on the rest of the plates. Use the hole punch to create holes on the outside edge of the plate to tie the yarn around to hold the mask on your head. You'll need to prepare the yarn ahead of time, too.

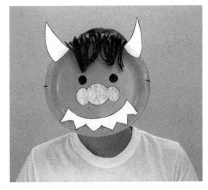

Figure 10.9 Wild Thing mask

During the program
- Have the children cut out horns, nose, and teeth.
- Have them glue the horns, nose, teeth, and hair (yarn) on the mask to create a Wild Thing.
- Using the 24-inch length of yarn, have the children tie the masks around their heads.

Directions for Wild Thing Feet
- Have the children cut out the monster feet. (You can resize the templates on legal-size paper to have larger feet on hand.)
- Have them cut the U-shaped line to create a flap to fit their feet in.

- Have them glue the yarn on the feet.
- Have them pull the U-shaped flap up and insert each foot to create a Wild Thing monster.

Music (2 minutes)

"Do the Monster Stomp," from *Playhouse Disney: Music Play Date* (Walt Disney Records, 2009)

- Be a monster while dancing to this song.

BOOKS TO DISPLAY

Burfoot, Ella. *Darkness Slipped In*. Roaring Brook Press, 2008.

Emberley, Adrian, Ed Emberley, and Rebecca Emberley. *There Was an Old Monster!* Orchard Books, 2009.

Fenton, Joe. *What's Under the Bed?* Simon and Schuster, 2008.

Hicks, Barbara Jean. *Jitterbug Jam*. Farrar, Straus and Giroux, 2005.

Hicks, Barbara Jean. *Monsters Don't Eat Broccoli*. Knopf Books for Young Readers, 2009.

Kontis, Alethea. *Alpha Oops: H Is for Halloween*. Candlewick, 2010.

Krosoczka, Jarrett J. *Annie Was Warned*. Alfred A. Knopf, 2003.

Landa, Norbert. *The Great Monster Hunt*. Good Books, 2010.

Lund, Deb. *Monsters on Machines*. Harcourt, 2008.

Murphy, Stuart J. *Monster Musical Chairs*. HarperCollins, 2000.

Sendak, Maurice. *Where the Wild Things Are*. HarperCollins, 1988.

Creepy Crawler Club (Grades 3–4)

Program Publicity

Have you ever wondered what type of monsters live under your bed? Learn about them at the XYZ Library this month. Create shadow puppets, monster mashups, and a mask while listening to stories about monsters during the month of October. For more information, call the library or register online.

WEEK ONE

Reading Component (10 minutes)

I Need My Monster by Amanda Noll (Flashlight Press, 2009)
- Ethan tests out temporary monsters while his usual monster is on vacation.

Activity: Monster under Ethan's Bed (15 minutes)

Supplies
- copies of figure 10.10 (one per child)
  Download full-size pattern from www.alaeditions.org/webextras
- 8.5-by-11-inch construction paper (one per child)
- scissors
- crayons, colored pencils, or markers
- glue

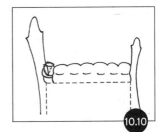

Directions
- Have the children make two vertical cuts on the dotted lines at the bottom of Ethan's bed.
- Have them fold the bottom of the bed up on the dotted line.
- Have them glue Ethan in his bed onto a piece of construction paper, leaving the flap under his bed free of glue.

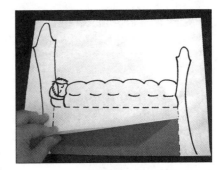

Figure 10.11 Ethan's bed

- Have them create their own monsters using crayons, colored pencils, or markers.

Music (3 minutes)

"Five Little Monsters" by Kiddle Karoo, from *Silly Monster House Party* (Silly Monsters, 2010)
- Act out this silly song that parodies "Five Little Monkeys."

WEEK TWO

Reading Component (5 minutes)

The Dark, Dark Night by M. Christina Butler (Good Books, 2008)
- The animals think there's a pond monster, but it's only their shadows!

Activity: Shadow Puppets (25 minutes)

Supplies
- copies of figure 10.12 (one per child)
- copies of figure 10.13 (one per child)
  Download full-size patterns from www.alaeditions.org/webextras
- scissors
- craft sticks (four per child)
- tape

Directions
- Cut out the four "pond monsters." Some of the monsters are very detailed. Just ask the children to cut out a rough outline of the monsters.
- Tape each "pond monster" to a craft stick.
- Let the children take turns telling the story to their neighbors at their table.

Music (2 minutes)
"Monster Hoe Down," from *Playhouse Disney: Music Play Date* (Walt Disney Records, 2009)
- Claw left, jump right, growl, and spin in this fast-paced country tune.

WEEK THREE

Reading Component (5 minutes)
Lunch Walks among Us (Franny K. Stein: Mad Scientist series) by Jim Benton (Spotlight, 2003)
- Read chapter 7, when Franny transforms into an average, nice girl.

Activity: Monster Mash-Up Flip Book (25 minutes)
Supplies
- copies of figure 10.14 (one per child)
- copies of figure 10.15 (one per child)
- copies of figure 10.16 (one per child)
  Download full-size patterns from www.alaeditions.org/webextras
- scissors
- crayons, colored pencils, or markers
- stapler

 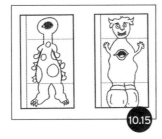 

Directions
- Have the children cut out the pages of the Monster Mash-Up book.
- Have them place the pages on top of each other to create a book, leaving the Frankenstein-style monster as the bottom page.
- Have them make two horizontal cuts on the remaining monster pages to create a flip book.

Music (4 minutes)

"Do the Monster" by Brainy Tunes, from *The Chills: Creepy Songs for Courageous Kids* (Ira Marlowe/Slow Reveal Music, 2009)
- Act like Franny while doing the "monster" in this song to end your program.

WEEK FOUR

Reading Component (5 minutes)

The Boy of a Thousand Faces by Brian Selznick (HarperCollins, 2000)
- A ten-year-old boy whose birthday is on Halloween is obsessed with monsters in this wonderfully illustrated story.

Activity: Mask Making (25 minutes)

Supplies
- grocery paper bags and/or dinner-sized paper plates (one per child)
- crayons, colored pencils, or markers
- googly eyes (two per child)
- yarn or string cut to 28-inch lengths (one per child)
- pom-poms
- feathers
- chenille stems
- glue
- scissors
- hole punch
- any other craft supplies you may have

Directions
- Put the craft supplies out and allow the children to use their imaginations to create their own mask using either a paper bag or a paper plate.
- Decorate with the various craft supplies you have in your cabinet.

Music (3 minutes)

"Monster Mash" by Bobby Boris Pickett, from *The Original Monster Mash* (Deca Music Group Unlimited, 1991)
- Dance around the room in slow motion while showing off your new mask.

BOOKS TO DISPLAY

Benton, Jim. *Lunch Walks among Us.* Spotlight, 2003. (This is one of many in the Franny K. Stein series.)

Butler, M. Christina. *The Dark, Dark Night.* Good Books, 2008.

Gaiman, Neil. *The Wolves in the Walls.* Harper Trophy, 2005.

Noll, Amanda. *I Need My Monster.* Flashlight Press, 2009.

Schwartz, Alvin. *Scary Stories Treasury: Three Books to Chill Your Bones.* Harper-Collins, 1985.

Selznick, Brian. *The Boy of a Thousand Faces.* HarperCollins, 2000.

Steer, Dugald A. *Monsterology: The Complete Book of Monstrous Beasts.* Candlewick, 2008.

Thaler, Mike. *The Class Trip from the Black Lagoon.* Spotlight, 2002. (This is one of many in the Black Lagoon series.)

Mask Making Club (Grades 5–6)

Program Publicity

Come to the XYZ Library and create a papier-mâché mask to use for your Halloween costume. Each week you'll layer your mask with papier-mâché and paint, creating a one-of-a-kind mask by the end of the month. Listen to booktalks about popular fiction such as *A Tale Dark and Grimm, The Monsters of Morley Manor, Dying to Meet You,* and *Something Upstairs.* Share scary stories while creating your mask. Please register for this program by (date) so the library can purchase enough materials for all participants.

Note: This program will require some room to keep the masks each week. If you have a basement area or a cabinet you can use, that would be ideal for the month.

WEEK ONE

Reading Component (5 minutes)

A Tale Dark and Grimm by Adam Gidwitz (Dutton, 2010)
  - Read the introduction about Hansel and Gretel in this dark comedy for children.

Activity: Mask Making (25 minutes)

Supplies
  - newspaper (enough to cover your tables with and for each child to papier-mâché with)
  - paper bowls (one per child)
  - balloons (one per child)
  - white glue
  - water

Directions
  - Have each child blow up a balloon to match the size of his or her face.
  - Have the children mix together a papier-mâché solution of half water and half white glue in a paper bowl.
  - Have them tear strips of newspaper about one to two inches in width. (If you use scissors or a paper cutter, the pieces of paper won't lay as smooth as torn pieces.)
  - Have them soak a strip of newspaper in the papier-mâché solution and place it on the balloon. They will layer half of the balloon with strips of newspaper to create the foundation for a mask.
  - Optional: Create a couple extra masks while the children are working on their masks. This way you'll be able to provide a mask for a child who joins your club late.

Background Music

Kidz Bop Halloween by Kidz Bop Kids (Razor and Tie, 2008)
  - "Thriller," the *Addams Family* theme, and "Nightmare on My Street" are a few covered by kids on this album.

WEEK TWO

Reading Component (5 minutes)

The Monsters of Morley Manor by Bruce Coville (Harcourt, 2001)
- Read pages 6–12, when Sarah and Anthony walk through Morley Manor for the first time.

Activity: Mask Making (25 minutes)

Supplies
- newspaper (enough to cover your tables with and for each child to papier-mâché with)
- paper bowls (one per child)
- white glue
- water

Directions
- Create more papier-mâché layers on your mask this week. For latecomers, use the extra masks you made last week.

Background Music

Spooky Wooky Halloween by Kidzone (CYP, 2010)
- The *Munsters* and *Ghostbusters* themes are featured on this CD.

WEEK THREE

Reading Component (5 minutes)

Dying to Meet You (43 Old Cemetery Road series, book 1) by Kate Klise (Houghton Mifflin, 2009)
- Read pages 45–51, where Seymour Hope, Ignatius B. Grumply, and E. Gadds are writing letters back and forth about a ghost named Olive living in the attic of the house.

Activity: Decorate Masks (25 minutes)

Supplies
- hole punch
- yarn or string cut to 28-inch lengths (one per child)
- paint
- paintbrushes
- scissors

Directions
- Have the children punch holes on the edges of the mask near their ears.
- Have them tie yarn or string in the holes to hold the mask on.
- Have them cut out eye holes using scissors.
- Have them decorate the masks using paint.

Background Music
Halloween by Countdown Kids (Suite, 2011)
- "Men in Black," "Purple People Eater," and "Werewolves of London" are sung by children on this album.

WEEK FOUR

Reading Component (5 minutes)
Something Upstairs by Avi (Avon Books, 1988)
- Read pages 12–16, when Kenny first meets the ghost.

Activity: Finish Masks (25 minutes)
Supplies
- paint
- paintbrushes

Directions
- Have the children put the finishing touches on their masks.

Background Music
Creepy: Songs, Music, and Sound Effects by Kidzone (CYP, 2010)
- These spooky sound effects will have the kids looking for the ghost Kenny met!

BOOKS TO DISPLAY

Avi. *Something Upstairs*. Avon Books, 1988.

Coville, Bruce. *Jeremy Thatcher, Dragon Hatcher*. Sandpiper, 2007. (This is one of many in the Magic Shop series.)

Coville, Bruce. *The Monsters of Morley Manor*. Harcourt, 2001.

Gaiman, Neil. *Coraline*. Harper Festival, 2008.

Gaiman, Neil. *Graveyard Book*. HarperCollins, 2008.

Gidwitz, Adam. *A Tale Dark and Grimm*. Dutton, 2010.

Klise, Kate. *Dying to Meet You*. Houghton Mifflin, 2009. (This is one of many in the 43 Old Cemetery Road series.)

Chapter 11

Boys Only

EACH YEAR YOUR GOALS CHANGE IN THE CHILDREN'S DEPARTMENT. YOU MAY need to market your programs to get more boys into the library, or to appeal to reluctant readers. This chapter will help you with ideas to appeal to boys of all ages.

Superhero Club (Grades K–2)

Program Publicity

It's a bird, it's a plane . . . no, it's Super You! Come to the XYZ Library and create a super version of yourself. Listen to superhero stories while creating your own superhero mask, cape, and ring, as well as a mix-and-match book.

WEEK ONE

Reading Component (5 minutes)
Mighty Max by Harriet Ziefert (Blue Apple Books, 2008)
  – Max likes to imagine he's different superheroes during his day at the beach.

Activity: Mixed-Up Heroes (25 minutes)

Supplies
- copies of figure 11.1 (one per child)
- copies of figure 11.2 (one per child)
- copies of figure 11.3 (one per child)
  Download full-size patterns from www.alaeditions.org/webextras
- crayons, colored pencils, or markers
- scissors
- stapler

  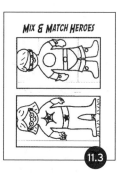

Directions
- Have the children color the superheroes using crayons, colored pencils, or markers. They can then cut out each page using scissors, leaving the hero with no dotted lines as the last page.
- Have them staple the book together, using four staples.
- Have them cut the dotted lines and mix up the heroes by folding the pages.

Music (3 minutes)

"Jump and Fly" by Laurie Berkner, from *Rocketship Run* (Two Tomatoes Records, 2008)
- Let the kids act out their favorite superhero. Or, if you have a parachute and scarves, you can assign a blue scarf to the "bad guy" and red scarf to the "good guy" and try to bounce the bad blue scarf out of the parachute.

WEEK TWO

Reading Component (5 minutes)

You Can Do Anything, Daddy! by Michael Rex (Putnam, 2007)
- A boy and his father tell an adventurous bedtime story together that includes run-ins with pirates and aliens.

Activity: Make Your Own Ring (25 minutes)

Supplies
- 2 cups of flour
- 1 cup salt
- ½–¾ cup water
- measuring cup
- mixing bowl
- food coloring (optional)

Directions
- You can create homemade salt dough ahead of time, or you can mix it up in front of the children so they know how to make it. This recipe can air-dry, so you don't need an oven to bake the rings. The children can take the rings home and let them dry overnight.
- Mix the flour and salt together in the mixing bowl. Slowly add ½ cup of water.
- Knead the dough. If it's too dry slowly add more water.
- If you want to color the dough, use food coloring.
- You can divide the dough into quarters and create four colors with food coloring.
- Hand out a small ball to each child so he can shape his own superhero ring.

Music (3 minutes)

"Superhero" by Milkshake Music, from *Play!* (Milkshake Music, 2007)
- Play a game of Follow the Leader with "Superhero" playing. Raise your rings high, low, to the side, in a circle.

WEEK THREE

Reading Component (5 minutes)

Captain Raptor and the Space Pirates by Patrick O'Brien and Kevin O'Malley (Walker Books for Younger Readers, 2007)
- This comic-book style picture book is a perfect mix of adventure and saving the day.

Activity: Mask (25 minutes)

Supplies
- copies of figure 11.4 (each sheet makes two crafts; one craft per child)
  Download full-size pattern from www.alaeditions.org/webextras
- crayons, colored pencils, or markers
- yarn or string cut to 28-inch lengths (one per child)

Directions
  - Have the children decorate their superhero masks using crayons, colored pencils, or markers.
  - Using the piece of yarn or string, have the children tie on the mask to fit their heads.

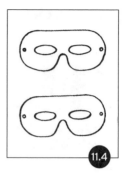

Music (3 minutes)
"Zero the Hero Number Stomp" by Dr. Jean, from *Just for Fun!* (Melody House Publishing, 2007)
  - Stand in a circle and clap out the numbers from one to one hundred in your superhero mask. Stomp and strike superhero poses in between each set of tens.

WEEK FOUR

Reading Component (10 minutes)
Batman: The Story of the Dark Knight by Ralph Cosentino (Viking Juvenile, 2008) or *Superman: The Story of the Man of Steel* by Ralph Cosentino (Viking Juvenile, 2010)
  - Learn the origins of Bruce Wayne and Clark Kent in these picture books.

Activity: Cape (25 minutes)
Supplies
  - 84-inch round vinyl tablecloths in various colors (each tablecloth makes four capes; one cape per child)
  - foam stickers or permanent markers to decorate (washable markers won't stay on)
  - Velcro tabs or clothespins for fastening

Directions
Ahead of time: Create capes from round tablecloths using the instructions found in figure 11.5 (download full-size pattern from www.alaeditions.org/webextras).
During the program: Let the heroes decorate capes using foam stickers and permanent markers.

Use Velcro strips or clothespins to fasten the capes at the neck. (Clothespins are cheaper to purchase and are easier to escape from if a villain catches you!)

Music (3 minutes)

"Super Hero Day" by Kimmy Schwimmy, from *The Imaginary World of Kimmy Schwimmy* (Ow Wee Music, 2010)
   – Parade around in your new cape acting out different superheroes highlighted in this song: Superman, Spider-Man, the Incredible Hulk, Wonder Woman.

BOOKS TO DISPLAY

Alborough, Jez. *Super Duck*. Kane/Miller Book Publishing, 2009.

Buehner, Caralyn. *Dex: The Heart of a Hero*. HarperCollins, 2007.

Cosentino, Ralph. *Batman: The Story of the Dark Knight*. Viking Juvenile, 2008.

Cosentino, Ralph. *Superman: The Story of the Man of Steel*. Viking Juvenile, 2010.

Cosentino, Ralph. *Wonder Woman: The Story of the Amazon Princess*. Viking, 2011.

Cottringer, Anne. *Eliot Jones, Midnight Superhero*. Tiger Tales, 2009.

Davis, David and Jacky. *Ladybug Girl and the Bug Squad*. Dial, 2011. (This is one of many in the Ladybug Girl series.)

Grey, Mini. *Traction Man Is Here*. Random House, 2008. (This is one of many in the Traction Man series.)

MacDonald, Ross. *Another Perfect Day*. Roaring Brook Press, 2002.

O'Brien, Patrick, and Kevin O'Malley. *Captain Raptor and the Moon Mystery*. Walker Books for Younger Readers, 2005.

O'Brien, Patrick, and Kevin O'Malley. *Captain Raptor and the Space Pirates*. Walker Books for Younger Readers, 2007.

Rex, Michael. *You Can Do Anything, Daddy!* Putnam, 2007.

Ziefert, Harriet. *Mighty Max*. Blue Apple Books, 2008.

Secret Identity Club (Grades 3–4)

Program Publicity

It's a bird, it's a plane . . . no, it's Super You! Learn about the secrets to becoming a true superhero. Study stories and create your own mythology, including a motive, a cover career, and secret headquarters. Play superhero games including Pass the Kryptonite, Spider-Man's Web, and Batcave Bombers. The secret meeting will be held at the XYZ Library. Secret code word: kryptonite.

WEEK ONE

Reading Component (10 minutes)

Superhero ABC by Bob McLeod (HarperCollins, 2008)
   – This ABC book features heroes of all abilities to awe your children with.

Activity: Choose a Superhero Power (15 minutes)

Supplies

   – copies of figure 11.6 (one per child)
      Download full-size pattern from
      www.alaeditions.org/webextras
   – crayons, colored pencils, or markers

THE ABCS OF A SUPERHERO

Directions

   – Give the children time to think of their one true superpower. Use the handout as a guide.
   – Go around the room and let the heroes introduce themselves and their new power.

Music: Pass the Kryptonite Game (10 minutes)

"Superman" by Danny Elfman. Comic Strip Heroes: Music From Gotham City and Beyond. (Silva America, 2006).
   – In addition to having a stereo to start and stop a song, you'll need something green to play this game. You can use a green Styrofoam floral ball, a green bouncy ball, or even a green piece of colored construction paper crumbled into a ball to use as kryptonite. Have the kids form a circle while standing. When the music starts, pass the kryptonite in a clockwise motion. Whoever is holding the kryptonite when the music stops is "out." Keep the kryptonite going until one hero is left. You can use this game to dismiss the children in a more orderly fashion, or you can use this as a transition from reading to activity time.

WEEK TWO

Reading Component (5 minutes)

Atomic Ace (He's Just My Dad) by Jeff Weigel (Perfection Learning, 2004)
- This rhyming story describes the challenges of having a famous super-hero father.

Activity: Superhero and Supervillain Identities (25 minutes)

Supplies
- copies of figure 11.7 (one per child)
- copies of figure 11.8 (one per child)
  Download full-size patterns from www.alaeditions.org/ webextras
- crayons, colored pencils, or markers

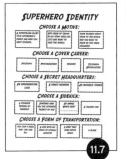
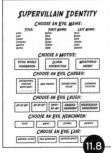

Directions
Allow the heroes to have time to discuss their new identities. Give them each a hero and a villain handout and let them choose their paths. Allow time for each child to read something aloud.

Music (5 minutes)

"Spider-Man," from *Comic Strip Heroes: Music from Gotham City and Beyond* (Silva America, 2006)
- You'll need a ball of yarn for this game. Stand in a circle and pass the ball of yarn across the circle to create Spider-Man's web. Tell the children they have to create the web before the song is over. At the end, have the kids hold the yarn tight while you toss a stuffed animal or puppet from your story-time collection into the web to see if it "sticks" without falling to the ground.

WEEK THREE

Reading Component (5 minutes)

Shredderman: Secret Identity by Wendelin Van Draanen (Yearling, 2006)
- Read pages 1–6, where Bubby Bixby is described as the villain of the story.

Activity: Superhero Logo (15 minutes)

Supplies
- copies of figure 11.9 (one per child)
  Download full-size pattern from www.alaeditions.org/webextras
- crayons, colored pencils, or markers

Directions
- Have the children create a logo for their superhero using crayons, colored pencils, or markers.

Music (10 minutes)

Batman: Original Motion Picture Score by Danny Elfman (Warner Brothers, 1989)
- You'll need a paper airplane (preferable made out of black paper to mimic the Batmobile) and painter's tape for this game. Tape an X on the floor about ten feet on the other side of the room. Tape a line on the floor so the children must stand behind it. Give each child a chance to throw the paper airplane as close to the X as possible. Play "The Batman Theme," "The Bat Cave," and "Charge of the Batmobile" as background music.

WEEK FOUR

Reading Component (5 minutes)

The Great Cape Rescue by Phyllis Shalant (Dutton Juvenile, 2007)
- Read pages 61–71, including the oath. Read the oath to everyone and have the children take it together.

Activity: Create Your Own Superhero Adventures Booklet (25 minutes)

Supplies
- copies of figure 11.10 (one per child)
- copies of figure 11.11 (each copy makes two crafts after it's cut vertically on the solid black line; one craft per child)
- copies of figure 11.12 (each copy makes two crafts; one craft per child)
- copies of figure 11.13 (each copy makes two crafts; one craft per child)
- copies of figure 11.14 (each copy makes two crafts; one craft per child)
  Download full-size patterns from www.alaeditions.org/webextras
- scissors
- stapler
- crayons, colored pencils, or markers

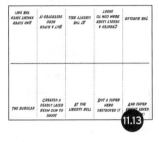

Directions

- If you think your group of kids won't be able to create these themselves, recruit volunteers to assemble them ahead of time.
- Have the children fold figure 11.10 in half to create the cover of the booklet.
- Have them place one page of figures 11.11, 11.12, 11.13, and 11.14 inside the cover and use five staples along the top edge.
- Have them cut on the dotted vertical lines to create a mix-and-match booklet.
- Have the children use crayons, colored pencils, or markers to create superhero adventures.

Background Music

Comic Strip Heroes: Music from Gotham City and Beyond by Danny Elfman (Silva America, 2006)

BOOKS TO DISPLAY

McLeod, Bob. *Superhero ABC*. HarperCollins, 2008.

Pilkey, Dav. *The Adventures of Captain Underpants*. Blue Sky Press, 2002.

Reynolds, Aaron. *Superhero School*. Bloomsbury, 2009.

Scieszka, Jon. *SPHDZ Book 1!* (Spaceheadz series). Simon and Schuster, 2011.

Shalant, Phyllis. *The Great Cape Rescue*. Dutton Juvenile, 2007.

Van Draanen, Wendelin. *Shredderman: Secret Identity*. Yearling, 2006. (This is one of many in the Shredderman series.)

Weigel, Jeff. *Atomic Ace (He's Just My Dad)*. Perfection Learning, 2004.

Graphic Novel Club (Grades 5–6)

Contributed by Amelia Yunker, Youth and Teen Services Librarian, Hudson Library and Historical Society, Hudson, Ohio

Program Publicity

Are you a big fan of graphic novels? Learn about the art at XYZ Library. Compare and contrast novels and their graphic counterparts, and examine the use of color and dialogue in comics. We'll have a Graphic Novel Reception the final week to share our work. For more information, go to www.xyzlibrary.org.

> If you have an overhead projector or scanner/laptop/projector, it would be best to scan in the following pages of the books so everyone can see. If you don't have these available to you, you can first read the pages then pass around the books. Or, you can photocopy the pages and make booklets for the kids.

WEEK ONE

Reading Component (15 minutes)
Kristy's Great Idea by Ann M. Martin (Scholastic, 1986)
  – Read pages 25–29.
Kristy's Great Idea: A Graphic Novel by Ann M. Martin (Graphix, 2006)
  – Read pages 40–45.

Activity: Discussion on the Difference between Novels and Graphic Novels (15 minutes)
Discuss the following questions:
  – Which version do you like better? Why?
  – Which version gives you more information?
  – Which cover of the book do you prefer? Why? Which cover displays the girls more accurately?
  – What do you think about the books being republished as graphic novels?
  – Which books do you think your parents or teachers would want you to read? Why?
  – Would you switch over to the text version if the series wasn't available as graphic novels?

Activity: Create a Graphic Novel (15 minutes)
Provide text and graphic versions of book series for children to look through. Some examples are Geronimo Stilton, Warriors, Baby Sitters Club, Hardy Boys,

Nancy Drew, and Scooby Doo. After browsing and getting ideas, have the children choose a section of a book to turn into a graphic novel. Either they can check out the books to work on their idea at home, or you can keep the books at the library for the next meeting.

Background Music
Iron Man Soundtrack by Ramin Djawadi (Lion's Gate Records, 2008)

WEEK TWO

Reading Component (15 minutes)
Robot Dreams by Sara Varon (First Second, 2005)
- Choose any section to read.

The Invention of Hugo Cabret: A Novel in Words and Pictures by Brian Selznick (Scholastic, 2007)
- Read pages 63–80.

Diary of a Wimpy Kid: Greg Heffley's Journal by Jeff Kinney (Amulet, 2007)
- Read pages 167–78.

Activity: Discussion on Dialogue (15 minutes)
Discuss the following questions:
- Which book is most like a graphic novel? How do the techniques of each book vary?
- Which book do you think expresses the most?
- They say "a picture is worth a thousand words." Do you agree or disagree, and why?
- What clues do the illustrators use in their drawings to let you know what's going on when there aren't any words?
- Could you remove the text or pictures and still know what was going on in the story?
- How do the drawings of *Diary of a Wimpy Kid* differ from *The Invention of Hugo Cabret*? Did you know that *Hugo Cabret* won the Caldecott Award for its illustrations? Do you think *Wimpy Kid* could win an award for its illustrations? Why or why not? Does it matter?

You can photocopy a page from a book and white-out the dialogue to see if the kids can still "read" the story. Try another page and white-out the pictures to see if the page can still be "read."

Activity: Create a Graphic Novel (15 minutes)

Supplies
- white copy paper (multiple sheets per child)
- pencils
- colored pencils

Directions
- Have the children use pencils and colored pencils to create a graphic novel on white copy paper.

Background Music

The Dark Knight Soundtrack by Hans Zimmer (Warner Records, 2008)

WEEK THREE

Reading Component (15 minutes)

Lunch Lady and the League of Librarians by Jarrett Krosoczka (Knopf, 2009)
- Read pages 1–8.

Babymouse: Queen of the World! by Jennifer Holm (Random House, 2005)
- Read pages 42–49.

Into the Volcano: A Graphic Novel by Don Wood (Blue Sky Press, 2008)
- Read pages 36 and 46.

Activity: Discussion on Color (15 minutes)

Discuss the following questions:
- When is color used?
- What feelings do you get when you look at black-and-white illustrations?
- What feelings do you get when you look at color illustrations?
- Have you ever tried to color using just one color?
- Why do you think the artist chose the color she did?

Choose an illustration from one of the books and make two copies: one in color and one in black-and-white. Let the kids discuss how each one makes them feel.

Activity: Finishing the Graphic Novel (15 minutes)

Supplies
- white copy paper (multiple sheets per child)
- pencils
- colored pencils

Directions
- Have the children use pencils and colored pencils to create a graphic novel on white copy paper.

Background Music

Batman Begins: Music from the Motion Picture by James Newton Howard and Hans Zimmer (Water Tower Music, 2005)

WEEK FOUR

Reading Component and Activity (45 minutes)

Have each child read their graphic novel aloud. You can open the program up to families so their parents and siblings can see their hard work.

Background Music

Music of DC Comics: 75th Anniversary Collection (Water Tower Music, 2010)

BOOKS TO DISPLAY

Boniface, William. *The Hero Revealed*. HarperCollins, 2008. (This is one of many in the Ordinary Boy series.)

Cody, Matthew. *Powerless*. Knopf, 2009.

Holm, Jennifer. *Babymouse: Queen of the World!* Random House, 2005.

Jinks, Catherine. *Evil Genius*. Graphia, 2008. (This is one of many in the Evil Genius series.)

Kinney, Jeff. *Diary of a Wimpy Kid: Greg Heffley's Journal*. Amulet, 2007. (This is one of many in the Diary of a Wimpy Kid series.)

Krosoczka, Jarrett J. *Lunch Lady and the League of Librarians*. Alfred A. Knopf, 2009.

Martin, Ann M. *Kristy's Great Idea*. Scholastic, 1986.

Martin, Ann M. *Kristy's Great Idea: A Graphic Novel*. Graphix, 2006.

Selznick, Brian. *The Invention of Hugo Cabret: A Novel in Words and Pictures*. Scholastic, 2007.

Varon, Sara. *Robot Dreams*. First Second, 2005.

Walden, Mark. *H.I.V.E.: Higher Institute of Villainous Education*. Simon and Schuster, 2008. (This is one of many in the H.I.V.E. series.)

Wood, Don. *Into the Volcano: A Graphic Novel*. Blue Sky Press, 2008.

Chapter 12

Girls Only

WHETHER IT BE A SUMMER READING OR SCHOOL VACATION SPECIAL, YOU MAY want to offer a girls-only program. This chapter will go above and beyond the tea party one-shot idea. Meet characters such as Fancy Nancy and Enola Holmes so you can introduce them to the girls of your community.

Fancy Nancy Club (Grades K–2)

Program Publicity

We're getting fancy—and you're invited! Join us for a Fancy Nancy extravaganza (that's a fancy word for *book club party*) during the month of (month). We'll create shimmery bookmarks, jeweled coronets (that's a fancy word for *tiara*), and ribbon streamers, and play elaborate games such as Explorer Relay and Musical Thrones. For more information, go to www.xyzlibrary.org.

WEEK ONE

Reading Component (7 minutes)

Fancy Nancy by Jane O'Connor (HarperCollins, 2005)
  – Meet Fancy Nancy, who loves to build her vocabulary while making everything in her universe extravagant.

Activity: Make Your Own Coronet (That's Fancy for Tiara) (25 minutes)

Supplies

- copies of figure 12.1 on pink, purple, and orange paper (one per child)
  Download full-size pattern from www.alaeditions.org/webextras
- construction paper in 2-by-12-inch strips, matching the colors of the tiaras (two per child)
- crayons, colored pencils, or markers (if you want to get really fancy, purchase glitter pens and jewel stickers)
- tape or glue

Directions

- Have the children cut out tiara and decorate it with crayons, colored pencils, or markers.
- Have them tape or glue two strips of construction paper to the tiara (one on each end).
- Have them tape the construction paper to fit their heads.

Music (3 minutes)

"Manners and Etiquette," from *Disney Princess Tea Party* (Walt Disney Records, 2005)

- Have the children line up with their new crowns on. Parade around the room as you curtsy and twirl.

WEEK TWO

Reading Component (5 minutes)

Fancy Nancy: Bonjour Butterfly by Jane O'Connor (HarperCollins, 2008)

- Fancy Nancy might miss her best friend's butterfly birthday party because of a family obligation.

Activity: Butterfly Bookmark (15 minutes)

Supplies

- copies of figure 12.2 on various colored paper or cardstock (one sheet makes two crafts; one craft per child)
  Download full-size pattern from www.alaeditions.org/webextras

- crayons, colored pencils, or markers
- scissors
- glitter pens and stickers (optional)

Directions
- Have the children cut out butterfly bookmark using scissors.
- Have them decorate it with crayons, colored pencils, or markers. Provide glitter pens and stickers if you have them.

Music: Musical Thrones (10 minutes)
"Musical Chairs," from *Disney Princess Tea Party* (Walt Disney Records, 2005)
- Arrange thrones (that's a fancy word for *chair*) in the center of the room, using one less throne than the number of players.
- Start the music.
- Players begin walking around the chairs.
- Stop the music.
- When the music stops, each child must find a seat. The child who doesn't find one is "out." Have them take a chair with them to the edge of one wall.
- Repeat until one person is left. Declare her Queen and have her begin the activity next week.

WEEK THREE

Reading Component (5 minutes)
Fancy Nancy: Explorer Extraordinaire by Jane O'Connor (HarperCollins, 2009)
- Fancy Nancy and her best friend, Bree, create their own Explorer's Club.

Activity: Ladybug Bracelet (10 minutes)
Supplies
- copies of figure 12.3 on red, pink, and purple paper (one copy makes three crafts; one craft per child)
  Download full-size pattern from www.alaeditions.org/webextras
- scissors
- crayons, colored pencils, or markers
- Velcro tabs to fit the bracelets on the girls' wrists

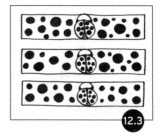

Directions
- Have the children decorate the ladybug bracelet using crayons, colored pencils, or markers.
- Have them cut out the bracelet using scissors.
- Have each child fit the bracelet on her wrist and place small pieces of Velcro on each end.

Music: Explorer Relay (15 minutes)

"Opening Race" by Randy Newman, from *Cars: The Original Soundtrack* (Walt Disney Records, 2006)

Supplies
- two borrowed suitcases, or two book boxes
- clock or stopwatch
- painters or masking tape
- various fancy clothes and explorer clothes (a total of ten to sixteen items; you can borrow these from staff and parents. Ideas include: tutu, tiara, baseball hat, watch, long sleeve shirt, long socks, bug net, clip-on earrings.)

Directions
- Fill each suitcase or box with an even amount of clothing items. You'll want to have between five and eight items in each.
- Use the painter's or masking tape to make two lines on the floor, which each team must stand behind.
- Put the suitcases or boxes on the other side of the room, or about ten feet away from the starting line.
- Divide the group evenly into two groups. If you have an uneven amount of kids, you can choose one to be timekeeper.
- Instruct the teams to send one child down to the suitcase/box and put on all the items. The child then returns to the starting line, takes off all the items, and lets the next child put them on. The next child races to the suitcase/box and takes all the items off. When she returns to cross the starting line, the next child races to the suitcase/box. Continue until each team member has a chance. The first team who finishes first wins.

WEEK FOUR

Reading Component (5 minutes)

Fancy Nancy and the Posh Puppy by Jane O'Connor (HarperCollins, 2007)
- Fancy Nancy doesn't agree with her family on the type of dog they should get.

Activity: Ribbon Streamers (25 minutes)

Supplies
- paper towel roll tubes (one per child)
- strips of various colored crepe paper cut to 20-inch lengths (ten strips per child)
- glue
- hole punch

Directions
- Have the children place glue on the outside of the paper towel tube.
- Have them wrap two strips of crepe-paper streamers around the paper towel tube.

Figure 12.4 Streamer example

- Have them punch eight holes in the bottom of the paper towel tube with the hole punch. (If you don't have enough hole punches for the group, you can do this step ahead of time.)
- Have them string the eight remaining streamers through the holes, tying a knot in each.

Music (5 minutes)

"Pinktastic" by John Gregor, from *Pinkalicious: The Musical* (Ghostlight, 2009)
- Dance with your new ribbon streamers.

BOOKS TO DISPLAY

Beaumont, Karen. *Shoe-La-La!* Scholastic, 2011.

Ferguson, Sarah. *Tea for Ruby*. Simon and Schuster, 2008.

Gay, Marie-Louise. *Stella*. Groundwood, 2004. (This is one of many in the Stella books.)

Henkes, Kevin. *Lilly's Big Day*. Greenwillow, 2006. (This is one of many in the Lilly books.)

Holabird, Katharine. *Angelina Ballerina*. American Girl, 2002. (This is one of many in the Angelina series.)

Kann, Victoria. *Pinkalicious*. HarperCollins, 2006. (This is one of many in the Pinkalicious series.)

O'Connor, Jane. *Fancy Nancy*. HarperCollins, 2005. (This is one of many in the Fancy Nancy series.)

O'Connor, Jane. *Fancy Nancy: Bonjour Butterfly*. HarperCollins, 2008.

O'Connor, Jane. *Fancy Nancy: Explorer Extraordinaire*. HarperCollins, 2009.

O'Connor, Jane. *Fancy Nancy and the Posh Puppy*. HarperCollins, 2007.

Primavera, Elise. *Louise and the Big Cheese*. Turtleback, 2011. (This is one of many in the Louise series.)

Rim, Sujean. *Birdie's Big-Girl Shoes*. Little, Brown Books for Young Readers, 2009.

Wilcox, Leah. *Falling for Rapunzel*. Puffin, 2005.

American Girl Club (Grades 3–4)

Most girls are familiar with the American Girl series. They know the historic characters and may even own a doll or two. Using the American Girl Today series, you can discuss modern problems that plague adolescents and growing up in this modern world.

Program Publicity

Get to know Mia, Kanani, Nicki, and Jess from the American Girl Today series. Read stories about girls your own age who are growing up and learning about the world. Create crafts with new friends, and enjoy new stories in the American Girl series. Join the club at the XYZ Library.

WEEK ONE

Reading Component (5 minutes)

Lanie by Jane Kurtz (American Girl Publishing, 2010)
   – Read pages 41–43, which describe the work that goes into a garden and how important it is to Lanie.

Activity: Plant a Seed (25 minutes)

Supplies
   – flowerpots (one per child; small ceramic pots or biodegradable peat moss pots)
   – potting soil
   – flower or herb seeds
   – foam stickers

Directions
Have the children decorate the flowerpots using foam stickers.
   – Have them fill the flowerpot about seven-eighths full with the potting soil.
   – Have them plant a seed in the middle of the pot according to the packet's instructions.

– Water the soil lightly before the children leave. (If the soil is wet, it won't fall apart too much on the car ride home.)

Background Music

Gonna Plant a Garden by Madeline L. Pots (Madeline L Pots Recordings, 2007)

WEEK TWO

Reading Component (5 minutes)

Nicki by Ann Howard Creel (American Girl Publishing, 2007)
  – Read pages 6–10, where Mom describes what a service dog is and how they help people.

Activity: Guest Speaker (25 minutes)

Contact your local animal shelter for a guest speaker to discuss service dogs with your club. The speaker can inform the children not only about service dogs, but also about what a shelter does for animals and how the children can help or volunteer.

WEEK THREE

Reading Component (5 minutes)

Aloha, Kanani by Lisa Yee (Pleasant Company Publications, 2011)
  – Read the first section of chapter 2, where Kanani picks flowers for Rachel's lei.

Activity: Hawaiian Lei (25 minutes)

Supplies
  – copies of figure 12.5 on pink, yellow, purple, green, and blue paper
    Download full-size pattern from www.alaeditions.org/webextras
  – string or yarn cut to 36-inch lengths (one per child)
  – solid-colored plastic straws cut to 2-inch lengths (about 3 straws per craft, or seventeen pieces per child)
  – scissors
  – hole punch
  – glitter pens (optional)

Figure 12.6 Lei example

Directions
- Have the children decorate the flowers with glitter pens.
- Have them cut out the flowers using scissors.
- With the hold punch, have the children put a hole in each center of the flower. (If you don't have enough punches for the group, this can be done ahead of time using a volunteer.)
- Have the children tie a knot at one end of the string or yarn and thread a flower to the end of the string. They thread a straw piece, then a flower, continuing until the string is filled.
- When the lei is filled, have the children tie the ends of the string together. The lei should slip over the children's heads without a problem.

Background Music
Hawaiian Playground by Putumayo Kids (Putumayo World Music, 2008)

WEEK FOUR

Reading Component (10 minutes)
Chrissa by Mary Casanova (American Girl Publishing, 2009)
- Read pages 7–13, where Chrissa has a hard time with her classmates in school.

Activity: Discussion about Bullying (25 minutes)
This is the perfect book to have a discussion about bullying. You can pose the questions "Have you ever been bullied? If so how did you deal with it?" The questions and answers in the back of the book are great to read aloud, too. You can show the girls the website www.randomactsofkindness.org and encourage them to do an act of kindness each day or each week. If they're really interested, you can encourage the girls to implement a Random Act of Kindness Week at their school.

BOOKS TO DISPLAY

Casanova, Mary. *Chrissa*. American Girl Publishing, 2009. (This is one of many in the American Girl series.)

Creel, Ann Howard. *Nicki*. American Girl Publishing, 2007.

Espeland, Pamela. *Making Choices and Making Friends*. Free Spirit Publishing, 2006.

Halpin, Mikki. *It's Your World—If You Don't Like It, Change It: Activism for Teenagers*. Simon Pulse, 2004.

Kaufman, Gershen. *Stick Up for Yourself: Every Kid's Guide to Personal Power and Positive Self-Esteem*. Free Spirit Publishing, 1999.

Kurtz, Jane. *Lanie*. American Girl Publishing, 2010.

Lewis, Barbara A. *The Kid's Guide to Service Projects: Over 500 Service Ideas for Young People Who Want to Make a Difference*. Free Spirit Publishing, 2009.

Small, Mary. *Way to Be! Learn How to Be Brave, Responsible, Honest, and an All-Around Great Kid*. Picture Window Books, 2010.

Yee, Lisa. *Aloha, Kanani*. Pleasant Company Publications, 2011.

Enola Holmes Secret Society Club
(Grades 5–6)

Contributed by Melissa Messner, Youth Services Librarian, Manhattan Beach Library, Los Angeles, California

Program Publicity

Join a secret, sassy society of Enola Holmes fans right here in XYZ Library. If you don't know about Enola, you should! Meet her in the series written by Nancy Springer. To know Enola is to love her. She is not just Sherlock Holmes's much younger little sister; she is a detective in her own right. You can celebrate the series and its star, Enola, starting (date).

WEEK ONE

Reading Component (10 minutes)
The Case of the Missing Marquess by Nancy Springer (Philomel Books, 2006)
From the moment we meet Enola in her very first book, she is trying to figure out who she is against the context of her missing mother. She is searching for clues about herself and what she should do. Read aloud pages 7–12 describing Enola's intense search of her mother's room looking for clues left by her mother just for her.

Activity: Journal Making (25 minutes)

Supplies
- notebooks; either buy composition books or create a notebook by stapling together computer paper with a construction paper cover (one per child)
- crayons, colored pencils, or markers
- glitter pens (optional)
- stickers (optional)
- feathers
- glue

Directions
- Have the children decorate the journals using crayons, colored pencils, markers, glitter pens, feathers, and glue.

Background Music

Lullaby by Jewel (Fisher Price, 2009)

WEEK TWO

Reading Component (10 minutes)

The Case of the Left-Handed Lady by Nancy Springer (Philomel Books, 2007)
- Read aloud pages 54–57 about Enola as she creates and uses one of her many fabulous disguises. Discuss perception and disguise.

Activity: Mask Making (25 minutes)

Supplies
- copies of figure 12.7 on cardstock or construction paper (each copy will make two crafts; one craft per child)
  Download full-size pattern from www.alaeditions.org/webextras
- scissors
- feathers
- glue
- glitter pens (optional)
- craft sticks

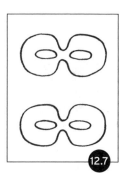

Directions
- Have the children cut out the masks using scissors.
- Have them decorate the masks using glue, glitter pens, and feathers.

– Have each child glue a craft stick to one side of the mask and hold it up in front of her face. Have them take turns using their new disguises.

Background Music

Phantom of the Opera: The Original Motion Picture Soundtrack by Andrew Lloyd Webber (Sony, 2005)

WEEK THREE

Reading Component (5 minutes)

The Case of the Bizarre Bouquets by Nancy Springer (Philomel Books, 2008)
– Read pages 44–47, describing one of the bouquets and one of the passages discussing flowers and their meanings.

Activity: Flower Bouquets (25 minutes)

Supplies
– copies of figure 12.8 on cardstock or construction paper in different colors (one copy makes four crafts; one craft per child)
– copies of figure 12.9 (one per child)
– copies of figure 12.10 (one per child)
  Download full-size patterns from www.alaeditions.org/webextras
– tissue paper in different colors (red, pink, blue, yellow, white)
– scissors
– green chenille stems
– glue

  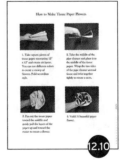

Directions
– If you have a relationship with a local florist or grocery store, you can ask them to donate fresh flowers for this craft. If not, you can create paper flowers to form a bouquet.

- Follow the instructions on figures 12.9 and 12.10 to create different flowers from construction and tissue papers. Have each child create a bouquet; encourage them to create a "message" with it.
- Allow enough time for each child to explain her creation. Have them share the bouquets with one another as they try to decipher each one collaboratively.

Background Music

Spring Symphony by Benjamin Britten (Deutsche Grammophon, 1997)

WEEK FOUR

Reading Component (5 minutes)

The Case of the Peculiar Pink Fan by Nancy Springer (Philomel Books, 2008)
- Read pages 37–40 describing pink objects.

Activity: Pink Diorama Picture Frames (25 minutes)

Supplies
- CD jewel cases (one per child)
- construction paper in shades of red, pink and white
- glue
- crayons, colored pencils, or markers
- glitter pens (optional)
- feathers
- jewel stickers (optional)
- lace (optional)
- optional: Take a picture of each participant (have pink props available such as a boa, a hat, gloves) and then print the pictures.

Directions
- Open up the CD jewel cases and have the children decorate one side to be a backdrop for a portrait using construction paper, crayons, colored pencils, markers, glitter pens, feathers, and jewel stickers.
- Have the children decorate the other side with their name in an acrostic poem using construction paper. For example, for Brenna:
  - Beautiful
  - Recycler
  - Elegant

- Nice
- Neat
- Artist

Background Music

The Best Baroque Album in the World . . . Ever! by George Frederick Handel
(EMI Classics, 2006)

BOOKS TO DISPLAY

Beccia, Carolyn. *The Raucous Royals: Test Your Royal Wits, Crack Codes, Solve Mysteries and Deduce Which Royal Rumors Are True.* Houghton Mifflin, 2008.

Chrisp, Peter. *A History of Fashion and Costume.* Volume 6, The Victorian Age. Facts on File, 2005.

Doyle, Conan. *The Adventures of Sherlock Holmes.* Dover Publications, 2009.

Post, Peggy. *Emily Post's the Guide to Good Manners for Kids.* HarperCollins, 2004.

Scoble, Gretchen. *The Meaning of Flowers: Myth, Language and Lore.* Chronicle Books, 1998.

Senning, Cindy Post. *Emily Post's Prom and Party Etiquette.* Collins, 2009.

Springer, Nancy. *The Case of the Bizarre Bouquets.* Philomel Books, 2008. (This is one of many in the Enola Holmes series.)

Springer, Nancy. *The Case of the Left-Handed Lady.* Philomel Books, 2007.

Springer, Nancy. *The Case of the Missing Marquess.* Philomel Books, 2006.

Springer, Nancy. *The Case of the Peculiar Pink Fan.* Philomel Books, 2008.

Swisher, Clarice. *Women of Victorian England.* Lucent Books, 2005.

Contributors

Cheryl Cox has been the children's librarian at Springfield Town Library in Springfield, Vermont, since 2001. She holds an MS in geology from the University of New Hampshire and taught math and science prior to pursuing her interests in children's literature.

Elizabeth Esposito works as a youth services librarian at South Huntington Public Library in Huntington Station, New York. She has a degree in library science from Long Island University.

Kerry Lemont is the youth services assistant at Brookfield Public Library in Brookfield, Illinois.

Melissa Messner earned her MLIS from UCLA in 2000. She is the children's services librarian at Manhattan Beach Library, which is part of the County of Los Angeles Public Library. She is thrilled to serve a dynamic audience of babies through teens, as well as the adults in their lives, through a rich array of programming and services.

Amelia Yunker completed her MLIS in one year from Eastern Michigan University. She got her start in libraries working concurrently at two libraries in southeast Michigan while regularly contributing to the Michigan Library Association. She has taken her enthusiasm and big ideas to Ohio, where she manages a Children's and Young Adult department at Hudson Library and Historical Society in Hudson, Ohio. You can find her blog and follow her reading at www.challengingthebookworm.wordpress.com.

Index